Successful Outsourcing and Multi-Sourcing

Successful Outsourcing and Multi-Sourcing

DEREK PARLOUR

GOWER

Gower Applied Business Research
Our programme provides leaders, practitioners, scholars and researchers with thought provoking, cutting edge books that combine conceptual insights, interdisciplinary rigour and practical relevance in key areas of business and management.

Published by
Gower Publishing Limited
Wey Court East
Union Road
Farnham
Surrey, GU9 7PT
England

Gower Publishing Company
110 Cherry Street
Suite 3-1
Burlington, VT 05401-3818
USA

www.gowerpublishing.com

British Library Cataloguing in Publication Data
A catalogue record for this book is available from the British Library

Library of Congress Cataloging-in-Publication Data
Parlour, Derek.
  Successful outsourcing and multi-sourcing / by Derek Parlour.
     pages cm
  Includes bibliographical references and index.
   ISBN 978-1-4724-2646-8 (hardback) -- ISBN 978-1-4724-2647-5 (ebook) -- ISBN 978-1-4724-2648-2 (epub) 1. Contracting out. I. Title.
  HD2365.P35 2014
  658.4'058--dc23
                                                                        2014015432

ISBN 9781472426468 (hbk)
ISBN 9781472426475 (ebk – PDF)
ISBN 9781472426482 (ebk – ePUB)

Printed in the United Kingdom by Henry Ling Limited, at the Dorset Press, Dorchester, DT1 1HD

Contents

List of Figures

About the Author

DEREK PARLOUR
Independent Outsourcing Consultant

Derek worked for National Rail Enquiries from 2002 to early 2014 and was involved in their transition from a purely call centre operation to a multi-channel business involving call centres, website, speech recognition, mobile internet, mobile applications, TV apps and text services, and dealing with over 500 million customer contacts each year. In addition, National Rail Enquiries have developed a B2B offering and now power over 300 different services that are presented to the customer under other brands.

This has involved a dramatic change in the shape of the business – moving the call centres to India and putting in place outsourcing agreements for other channels, as well as developing the commercial and contractual structure for delivering these services through multi-sourcing. At the same time, National Rail Enquiries have kept their team very small, with only 26 people employed directly.

The transformation from single-sourcing to multi-sourcing has involved a fundamental change in the approach, attitudes and structure at National Rail Enquiries and the experience gained, and lessons learnt, from that process form much of the basis for this book.

Prior to National Rail Enquiries Derek held a number of senior financial roles in outsource service providers mainly centred on business development and sales. These roles have largely been based outside the UK and in different industries, such as oilfield services and telecoms with Schlumberger (including Worldwide CFO for their Telecoms division), and contract catering and facilities management with Gardner Merchant (finally as regional CFO for SE Asia and Australia).

Derek now works as an independent consultant advising businesses on their outsourcing strategy and how to deliver that strategy.

Derek is a chartered accountant (FCMA) with an MSc in Strategic Management Accounting and is a member of the National Outsourcing Association Council.

Foreword

CHRIS SCOGGINS

CEO, National Rail Enquiries

"Outsourcing". What an emotive word that is in our society. So often linked to moving jobs offshore, to profiteering, to abdicating your responsibilities, etc. "I work in outsourcing" is not an introduction that guarantees a warm response at dinner parties.

But that is because there have been (and continue to be) many big or high profile examples of where outsourcing is blamed for failures in delivering good services. Outsourcing is hard work, it is not an easy option. It should make the organisation more effective as well as more efficient. It has the potential to deliver better services. But only when it is done properly diligently, and intelligently.

Outsourcing is something you have to think about very carefully – how can you make it fit with the culture of your organisation, with your business proposition to customers and clients, with the need to move quickly in today's markets to get ahead and stay there?

Derek and I have built our model of outsourcing gradually over a period of some years, and we were among the first to use a multi-sourcing model effectively. I would like to say that we sat back and worked out the whole model in one great exercise, probably in some whacky location in the mountains. But we did not, and I believe that where we have ended up is a better place than we could have achieved through a purely intellectual exercise. We felt our way through this new area of multi-sourcing, we made mistakes and we changed our approach as a result.

So this book gives you plenty of real experience, things that really worked and some that did not. And I am sure that we still have problems to uncover and that our approach will continue to evolve.

But I hope that it will be of some benefit to you the reader, whatever your role, and that you will be able to avoid some of the errors waiting for you out there.

This book also makes it very clear that you can outsource business functions but you cannot effectively outsource risk: if the function fails, it is your brand and your sales that suffer regardless of what the contract says! And I have yet to see a contract where the outsourcer guarantees to cover the true impact of this on your shareholder value.

Acknowledgements

There are so many people who have contributed to this book, either with their knowledge or unwittingly, it is impossible to list them all so apologies to any I may have missed out.

Everyone I have ever worked with, in the companies I have worked for and the companies I have worked with, has helped build up my experience and knowledge, helped me learn how to do things and, just as importantly, how not to do things.

Specifically I would like to mention my colleagues at Gardner Merchant, especially Graham Smith, Garry Hawkes and Rod Simpson, who gave me my first chance to work overseas in my early 20s. That put me way out of my comfort zone and meant the learning curve was a lot steeper than I could ever have hoped for, and it gave me an exposure to a wide range of disciplines – from bidding to strategy, from finance to legal and from tax to operations.

I would like to thank the people I worked with at Serco, as the joint venture with Serco taught me much about bidding outsourcing contracts, especially the treatment of risk, and working with their bid teams and seeing the methodology and discipline they employed was invaluable.

This was followed by the help I got from people at Schlumberger, where the big-company discipline and huge numbers involved in the oil business gave me further experience. It also was a very different environment with regard to client expertise and governance. Oil companies have people who really understand the services that companies such as Schlumberger deliver.

Lastly in experience I would like to thank the people at ATOC and National Rail Enquiries, especially Chris Scoggins, the CEO of National Rail Enquiries. Chris and I, together with the rest of the National Rail Enquiries team, worked on the transformation of National Rail Enquiries into the multi-sourcing award-winning business it is today. Without the support of Chris and the National Rail Enquiries team, much of what I have written about in this book would never have come to pass.

In general outsourcing there are so many authors, journalists and researchers who I have read and quoted it is impossible to name them all. However the work of the Institute for Government in analysing public sector outsourcing, the biggest growth area over the past few years, has proved invaluable and I am grateful for their permission to reproduce some of their work in this book.

There is also the National Outsourcing Association itself, who have kindly let me use their excellent Outsourcing Life Cycle to demonstrate a sound outsourcing framework, and many of the people in the NOA for their help and assistance.

Lastly there is everyone I have ever talked to about outsourcing, at work, conferences, seminars and through the UK National Outsourcing Association. Listening to and debating ideas from differing viewpoints and industries has helped shape my views on the subject and from there the contents of this book.

This book is, in part, co-written by all of the above.

PART I
What Do You Outsource and Why?

Nearly every company outsources to a degree. The question is: how far do you go? That is a strategic decision worthy of much thought and analysis and one not to be taken lightly.

Everyone has heard the horror stories about outsourcing. The poor services delivered, contracts going well over budget, huge IT developments never being delivered. It isn't all good news, and even allowing for the tendency of the press to report the bad over the good, there is no denying that it doesn't always work. However, it is a very widespread practice and is mostly successful.

A normal small company with less than ten people may not regard itself as outsourcing. However they are unlikely to clean their own offices, supply their own telecoms, support their software etc. They outsource these and, even at this level, outsourcing is growing.

Take the example of that small company, then move to National Rail Enquiries. This is a business running cutting-edge back office systems, a diverse selection of front-end customer-facing channels, B2B services and over 500 million contacts per year, plus passing on nearly £1 billion in sales leads to its shareholders. The demands of the National Rail Enquiries outsourcing model are constantly changing as customer needs change. However, the organisation employs less than 30 people. National Rail Enquiries outsources virtually everything and effectively operates as a procurement and contract management company whilst still controlling its overall strategy.

Many companies lie between these two examples, but why would you outsource in the first place? The outsourcing company is obviously charging a margin, so why not do it yourself and save the margin?

The answer lies in the outsourcer's expertise and size, but also in your own strategy and core competencies. So what do you need to look for in outsourcing, and what are the factors to take into account?

This part of the book, detailing the factors involved, is long and detailed. I make no apology for this as there are a number of factors to take into account when making the decision to outsource, although they don't all apply in all cases. Many of these factors have pluses and minuses, and you need to think these through before deciding on an outsourcing strategy or indeed whether outsourcing is for you at all. Suppliers equally need to understand the factors to enable them to meet clients' needs and concerns.

So to start with, why would you outsource in the first place? What are the benefits and what are the limitations around those benefits? What does an outsourcer offer, what are the downsides and what factors need to be taken into account? The answer to these questions depends on what you are outsourcing and what your overall strategy is, but the headings can be broadly split into Technological, Human, Strategic and Financial.

I will cover these headings in the following four chapters. Whilst it is true that the application of these factors depends on what is being outsourced, who the outsourcer is and what the client strategy is, it is always a good idea to consider the decision in as wide a context as you can. Just because it doesn't apply now, doesn't mean it won't apply in the future.

Chapter 1
Technological Factors

New Technology

Access to new technology is one of the desirable outcomes of outsourcing, and came sixth in a KPMG survey of Australian IT outsource contracts (Hurley and Schaumann 1997). In many cases it rates above cost.

Whilst it is a reasonably strong argument that a company with several clients will be able to afford, and have the expertise for, new technology (Hill 2000), it is also possible that, because they are working for several clients, the technology may not be ideal for the client's requirements and there may be a need to compromise. A balancing act is involved that may depend on how specialised the client's needs are. The impact of this factor varies with the complexity of the task. The technology requirements for simple tasks may naturally be lower and access to new technology may not be such an issue. However, in all cases this is something that needs consideration. Your current requirements may be for simple tasks but the opportunity to get access to technological advances without the capital outlay may bring about the opportunity for a change in approach and thinking.

This factor has particular resonance in these days of fast-moving technology, and is one of the factors behind the National Rail Enquiries outsourcing strategy. Many of the customers of National Rail Enquiries use the latest technology, so they need to meet their needs and have access to that technology at the customer-facing end of the business. On the back end of the business, they need to be able to meet the capacity requirements of an increasing appetite for information and the technology requirements for a wide variety of channels. We reached a decision that National Rail Enquiries needed to use third parties to get access to the technology in order to deliver what they wanted and what their customers need.

Avoiding Obsolescence

Following on from access to new technology comes the issue of obsolescence. This is a constant concern in IT and the increasing speed of change is only making this more of an issue, although the falling price of technology is a counterbalance to this. A survey of Spanish universities had 11.4 per cent citing the fear of obsolescence as a factor in outsourcing (Claver, Gonzalez, Gasco and Llopis 2002). There is a case for saying that outsourcing reduces this risk, in that it makes sense to have the supplier take the risk of obsolescence, although there is always a cost to this. However, yet again, the balancing act comes into play, as it may be better to have older technology that is specific to your needs than more up-to-date technology that isn't. Also, using the latest technology isn't always a good thing as it may not have been sufficiently tried and tested. The phrase "leading, not bleeding edge" was coined for this concern.

There is also a concern with outsourcing technology that it is difficult to keep technology up to date. It is easy at the start, but contractual requirements in this area are difficult to be specific with and therefore difficult to enforce. In long-term contracts, especially single-supplier ones, there is an obvious disincentive on the supplier to refresh technology, especially towards the end of the agreement. As highlighted above, this is difficult to hedge against; future technology is difficult to forecast, describe and price, and therefore difficult for the client to put in as a requirement and difficult for the supplier to cost. This is made worse by the length of the contract, since there is always an incentive to lengthen the contract where there is upfront capital spent by the supplier, so that the cost can be recovered without large annual charges to the client. The supplier is after an ongoing business relationship so there is a desire to keep up to date. Nonetheless, there has to be a balance between the factors of cost and ongoing efficiency which is, in any case, difficult to contract for.

Again this is a key driver for National Rail Enquiries. The fast-changing pace of technology means that they are always looking to upgrade both back-end and customer-facing systems. This makes obsolescence a real risk, but it isn't simply a case of passing the risk onto a supplier. If all the risk is put onto the supplier then the cost of that risk will be reflected in the supplier costs. The right approach is more a case of picking suppliers who are geared up to mitigate obsolescence by their approach to development. Suppliers who are looking to the future are better placed to help you meet the risk of obsolescence than those who are less forward thinking.

Disaster Recovery and Business Continuity

Another advantage of outsourcing technology, again mainly down to economies of scale and the concentration of expertise, is disaster recovery and business continuity. As part of the specialised and focused nature of the outsourcer (as well as this not being just part of their business but the core of their business), disaster recovery and business continuity procedures and systems are likely to be better with an outsourcer than the client who may not have the same scale, technology or investment (Law 1999; Hill 2000). The value of this factor will depend on how essential the service is: can it be down for a week, or a day, or is it essential to have 100 per cent availability? It also depends on the vulnerability of the service and it's susceptibility to denial of service attacks. Technology can help provide a resilient service with high availability if that is what you need.

In Chapter 12, which looks at the future of outsourcing, I discuss the changes that we have seen in the area of hosting that have greatly increased National Rail Enquiries' disaster recovery and business continuity capacity. The technology of cloud hosting can help organisations in this area, without huge investment, and give them huge capacity and resilience.

Specialist Skills

Under the heading of technology also comes access to specialist skills. A large IT outsourcer may well have specialist programmers and people with specific software skills that the client may not be able to support (Kakabadse and Kakabadse 2000; Hurley 2001). A client organisation with in-house IT facilities can of course buy in contract skills, but this can be more expensive and there is a greater risk of a loss of continuity in the use of contract staff. Outside of IT outsourcing suppliers can provide specialist skills that are difficult for a client to gain access to directly. Catering is one example of this where the training given to the staff mean that they are not just skilled in cooking but specifically skilled in running a staff cafeteria.

There is also the business benefit of specialist skills. The relative cost to an organisation of having average skills as opposed to specialist skills can make the difference between success and failure. The issue of specialist skills is more of a benefit in the case of large one-time projects, where the benefit of specialist skills can be greater and the need for long-term expertise less of a problem. On the other hand, there is always the risk that the supplier will reallocate the best staff to newer and more lucrative contracts, if needed, to the detriment of the original client (Hirschheim and Lacity 2000). Outsourcers may not have the same business targets as their clients and will put the best resource where it will help them meet their needs, rather than those of the client. To some extent this can be offset contractually with a "key personnel" clause (see Chapter 11 on minimising downside and maximising upside) but ultimately this is difficult to control.

However, skills aren't the only issue as an understanding of the client's business is also an important factor. A highly skilled person with little business knowledge may not be as good as a less skilled one who knows your business (Lacity and Hirschheim 1993).

This is another key factor to the National Rail Enquiries sourcing strategy. The technology that they use at the back end and that customers use at the front end not only use more advanced technology but more varied technology. National Rail Enquiries couldn't possibly hope to effectively maintain the specialist skills needed for these new technologies themselves, and so they turn to outsourcers. As well as reducing the cost of acquiring the specialist skills outsourcing also reduces the cost of getting rid of them. As technology moves on some lines become obsolete, but the cost to the client of losing the specialist skills that they have required just involves not renewing a service contract, rather than the whole process of redundancy and the issues surrounding it.

Implementation and Transition

In the area of technology implementation is key. Poor implementation can affect the life of a contract, as it impacts on effectiveness and benefit realisation, and it is an area where trust can be lost that is difficult to get back.

It is also an area where there are common failures and it needs to be planned carefully by both the supplier and the client. Generally speaking, the supplier selected should have substantial implementation experience and the client may wish to pay the supplier to take on most of the implementation work, although the client needs to retain a degree of control over this process (Law 1999). Whilst the supplier may have some expertise in this area, it is not one to be left to the supplier completely as they may not possess the industry knowledge that the client does. Moreover the client should not leave its business in the hands of a new supplier – or any supplier, for that matter.

The issues around implementation and control (referred to throughout this book but particularly in Chapter 10 on a suggested sourcing framework) demonstrate that there are many factors to be taken into account (Useem and Harder 2000). Sometimes they seem contradictory but it depends on the weight they are given. That will depend on circumstances.

Summary

A great deal of outsourcing today involves IT. In these areas it is obvious that the technological factors underlying the outsourcing decision are key. However, technology is playing a bigger part in more and more services so this chapter shouldn't be ignored, even if the service being outsourced isn't IT.

For example if the service being outsourced is courier services, the level of IT behind that service is important. Outsourcing a courier service can give you access to new technology, such as online tracking, that you may not have had access to before. It may also be that access to that technology is very cheap if the courier firm uses it across all its clients, and that the incremental cost to the outsourcer is negligible.

The catering industry also provides examples of this. You wouldn't normally associate catering with supplying better technology, but modern catering operations use a good deal of technology. Menus are planned ahead and the systems take the menu, break it down into the ingredients and place the orders for the food based on the menus. They also cost the menus and work out sale prices and portion sizes in order to meet gross margin targets. All this means that there is much more science in the ordering and costing process with the subsequent impact on cost control and margins. The benefit of these better controls ultimately helps the client.

In short, technology is all around us, so think about this area when outsourcing as you may find that it impacts on the most unlikely services.

Chapter 2
Human Factors

Clients are human, outsourcers are human and the customers are human. You ignore this area at your peril.

It is an area where legislation pays a particularly important part and has huge potential for public relations and political damage. Ask any company that has offshored a service about how the existing staff and wider stakeholder community react. Buying materials and components from overseas doesn't seem to make an impact on people's thinking, but outsource a service to an overseas company and you are likely to see concern about local jobs being lost and a perceived impact on service quality.

This chapter covers the human factors in outsourcing. This is a big area encompassing staffing, stakeholder and control issues.

Legislation Around the Transfer of Staff from One Employer to Another

In the UK legislation creates issues around staff. The Transfer of Undertakings (Protection of Employment) Regulations 2006 (TUPE) relates to the rights of staff when work is transferred between employers. It has had huge impacts on the outsourcing industry in the UK and is something that both clients and suppliers need to take into account when agreeing contracts. Clear statements as to whether TUPE applies and where the liability lies are essential. Although legislation places the liability on the supplier the client needs to understand the TUPE impact and may wish to use the contract to place liability where it is best controlled.

This isn't just a UK issue. TUPE, under other names and forms, also exists in other countries. For example the EU has the overriding legislation called the Acquired Rights Directive.

TUPE may mean that members of staff have to be transferred to the new contractor and this may negate some of the benefits of specialist skills that you expect to get from an outsourcer.

Whilst this isn't usually looked on as a strategic issue the legal terms need to be properly thought through to negate problems both in cost and human terms.

Quality of Staff

There is some argument that outsourcers can recruit and retain better quality staff. Mediocrity is not something that businesses strive for and in some areas can cause significant problems (Hurley 2001). The difference between just any performer and having someone at the top levels of performance can easily be the difference between a profitable and a loss-making business line.

Outsourcers can retain staff because of the specialised nature of their business. They can offer better career paths with a higher concentration of staff in the same business areas, as opposed to the client organisation where the number of people in the same business area is likely to be lower.

In addition, outsourcers' investment in better, more up-to-date technology will also help retain staff who wish to be working at the cutting edge, and outsourcers' staff can also benefit from working with different clients.

With the larger staff numbers a higher investment in training can be justified. Training is a big benefit for staff and can help in the area of staff retention.

However, clients should note that the career path and variety that an outsourcer offers staff very often means moving staff on between clients. Staff retention, whilst clearly a benefit to the outsourcer, may be a somewhat limited benefit from a client's point of view. Sometimes clients can be paying for outsourcing staff to gain new skills, and improve existing ones, only to have them moved off the account, either to win new business for the supplier, or to help retain other clients.

It really depends on the nature of the service as to whether the more specialised employees are required long term. Sometimes the specialist skills are only required for a short period of time; in this case the outsourcer may have more of the right type of people to step in. If the staff are required long term then the client may just have to accept that the supplier will move on good staff to continue their career progression and to benefit the outsourcer's business. A client can try to retain staff from the outsourcer on their account using key personnel clauses (see Chapter 11) but ultimately these may be of limited value. You can't force someone to stay when there are better opportunities elsewhere.

Staff Motivation

In a similar vein to staff quality there is the ability to motivate staff. Surveys have shown that staff, provided they are paid at least market rate, do not rate money as a high motivator (notably KPMG, in Hurley and Costa 2001). They are more motivated by better training, working in a cutting-edge environment and working in strong teams (Hurley 2001). These are things that the outsourcer may well be better placed to offer than the client organisation.

It has also been stated that motivation is better if corporate goals and strategies are known to staff and are aligned to staff objectives. However the mix of client and supplier goals adds a complication for staff in outsourcing organisations (Kakabadse and Kakabadse 2000).

Outsourcers have the environment to motivate staff but there needs to be a clear understanding of what objectives are and, as in many factors, the possible differences between client and supplier objectives adds a level of complication.

Control

Outsourcing inevitably leads to a reduction in the level of control that the client organisation has. Internal expertise will be transferred out and the client will have some degree of reliance on the supplier or suppliers. On top of this the staff no longer work directly for the client and may now be working on supplier premises (Law 1999). This all adds up to barriers between the client and the staff working on the client's business. However, the whole issue of control can very often be emotional rather than logical, and the desire to have complete control over everything is understandable but not always sensible. As I have pointed out before, just about every company outsources, they might not think of it that way but they do. Once you accept that you outsource, then comes the decision as to how far to go and control is usually a significant factor in this decision. However that discussion needs to be based on logic and sound business reasons rather than emotion.

That business decision depends to a great deal on what is being outsourced, who the supplier is, who the client is, what their strategy is and how the contract is negotiated. Losing a degree of control may not be a bad thing but it has to be at the level the client is happy with.

The whole area of control is a key factor to successful outsourcing and is one of the reasons why National Rail Enquiries have been so successful at outsourcing. We never gave up control of the overall service and the governance structure is designed to ensure we never lost our view of the individual elements of that service. That isn't to say it always works perfectly, but the whole ethos is to manage the suppliers who provide the services rather than hand over parts of the business to them.

In order to outsource your business processes to a third party you need to have effective skills in-house, not least of which is contract management. You cannot outsource and leave it to run itself – to extract the maximum benefit from any outsourcing arrangement the client must manage the relationship with the supplier, commercial, technical, service delivery, etc. in a structured and coordinated way. Much of the outsourcing framework discussed later in Chapter 10 is around the importance of governance.

The decision on how much control to give away is in the client's hands and they have to balance the level of vulnerability against the prospect of competitive edge. If there is a trade-off between flexibility and control it should be the client's decision on where that line is drawn.

Control over an outsourcing contract by a client can be achieved in various ways, and Langfield-Smith and Smith (2003) identified three different types of management control system in outsourcing arrangements and how these are applicable to different types of outsourcing contracts. The key criteria were: how programmable the tasks were, how easy it was to measure output, whether the specificity of the assets (people, equipment, site, etc.) made redeployment or alternative use difficult, and the level of repetition in the tasks to be performed under the arrangement.

- Market-based control is suitable where there is high task programmability, high measurability of output, low asset specificity and high task repetition. Measurement is easier and market forces help to control the supplier so management control systems (including the contract) do not need to be so strong to give efficient and effective output.

- Bureaucracy-based control is suitable where there is high task programmability, high measurability of output, medium asset specificity and low to medium repetitiveness. In this case controls will be more prescriptive involving detailed contracts, but there is still autonomy between the parties.

- Trust-based control is for where there is a low level of task programmability, low levels of measureable output, high asset specificity and the transactions are not highly repetitive. The risk and uncertainty of these situations make a trust-based control system better suited. The control systems are personal consultations and communication and are more informal under this type of arrangement. "Trust is necessary to achieve control as the activities and output cannot be measured with any certainty" (Langfield-Smith and Smith 2003). Because of the nature of our business, National Rail Enquiries use this type of control in most of our outsourcing arrangements.

This paper by Langfield-Smith and Smith highlights how control systems apply in different ways to different types of outsourcing contract. It cannot be the case that levels of control should be the same for all types of outsourcing arrangements. There will be some, at the market-based end, where not having much control over the contract doesn't matter, and there will be contracts at the other end of the scale where it definitely does. There is a strong relationship between partnership and outsourcing success but this does depend on what is being outsourced and, more particularly, where the service lies on the Langfield-Smith and Smith scale.

However, discussions on control inevitably come back to the contract. This is usually within the control of the client and the client can make the contract as strong or as weak as they like (Buffo 2004). However, the fear of losing control can result in restrictive contracts which may mean the client loses some of the flexibility that outsourcing can give. A pragmatic approach is to have the contract as strong as you need for the service being delivered (Langfield-Smith and Smith 2003).

The question of whether there can be a partnership in outsourcing has long been debated. Some believe that the profit motive makes real partnerships impossible and partnerships in outsourcing are likely to be based on loose agreements that may be exploited by the vendor. This can be especially true where there develops an asymmetry of resources and power in favour of the vendor (Willcocks 1994). However, whilst these are valid concerns, I believe that the client has the ability to negate these risks and create useful partnerships from outsourcing arrangements. Vested outsourcing and the change from "what's in it for me" to "what's in it for we" attitudes are growing (Vitasek, Nyden, and Frydlinger 2013), demonstrating that "win-win" isn't just a nice phrase. My experience would suggest that "win-win" is a reality.

Governance processes have come a long way since these studies were done; now the development of strategic and tactical outsourcing skills in the client's organisation goes a long way to negating these risks and, in addition, suppliers are becoming more long term in their thinking and not as likely to endanger a relationship for a quick buck.

Implementation

One of the most dangerous times in an outsourcing relationship is the beginning (Kakabadse and Kakabadse 2000). If it doesn't start right it is difficult to get back on track, so a good initial implementation is so important (PA Consulting 2001).

The first part of this is getting the client staff onside. Very often outsourcing is seen as a threat by client staff (and in many cases they are right) but getting the client staff to work with the supplier isn't impossible and will make the implementation or transition stage run much better. Financial incentives is the blunt way to do this but more subtle approaches, such as greater involvement of client staff in the process, should be considered.

Detailed planning is required so that the transition goes smoothly. Some people in the client organisation may think that outsourcing is a bad idea and may also feel threatened by the process. Poor planning will only reinforce those prejudices.

Communication is essential so that the clients staff know what is going on and the supplier understand the client's needs. You cannot expect the supplier to meet your needs if you don't let them know what your needs are!

This area isn't rocket science. It is just good project management but it comes back to the need for the client to have the right skillset in their own organization to oversee the implementation.

Stakeholder Buy-In

It is important that any outsourcing agreement has support from the stakeholders as far as is reasonably possible. If it is just a management decision to bring it in against other resistance then the chances of success are reduced. Adding client-side staff to the team helps encourage buy-in and improves the level of expertise available. Both of these will improve the chances of success (Goolsby 2003).

There are, however, limits to buy-in. It would be great if everyone could agree but not all stakeholders will have the same objectives, so getting agreement from everybody can be difficult or even impossible. The attempt should certainly be made but there comes a time when you just have to go ahead and deal with resistance as you go along.

Client Engagement

Alongside the stakeholder buy-in goes the level of client engagement. When dealing with human factors the client cannot simply stand back and let the supplier deal with any issues. The client needs to be there, fully engaged, from day one. This will be a main part of the discussion on successful outsourcing frameworks, but for now it is sufficient to look at the level of client engagement as one of the factors in outsourcing.

Summary

In a world of technology, processes and systems it is easy to overlook the human factors. They may not seem to be that important, and will almost always seem to require a high level of effort, so it is easy to put them to the back of your mind.

However, business is people, and any business decision that doesn't take into account human factors is taking a huge risk.

Chapter 3
Strategic Factors

Outsourcing is all about strategy. As I will cover in later chapters successful outsourcing needs an outsourcing strategy that is in line with the overall business strategy.

However, to align outsourcing strategy with business strategy you need to understand the strategic benefits and issues with outsourcing. Once you understand what the strategic factors are within outsourcing, you can then look at your outsourcing strategy in order to maximise the benefit of these factors within the framework of your overall business strategy.

In the following sections I highlight the main strategic factors that outsourcing can impact.

Time to Market

There is research to show that outsourcing improves product process life cycle times from initial idea to implementation. Best-in-class multi-sourcing should give greater depth and knowledge and offer better inputs (Drtina 1994; Quinn and Hilmer 1994). Outsourcing allows clients to buy in already developed technologies, reducing development time and taking a good deal of the risk out of the development.

However, time to market is not necessarily improved purely from the process. Knowledge of the company and an understanding of the market are also required and it may be that this is less solid in an outsourcing environment.

Whilst there is research that shows a correlation between faster speed to market and outsourcing, it is difficult to believe that this is the only factor affecting time to market. It is possible that outsourcing comes from a more dynamic and risk-taking management ethos. This could be a bigger contributor to the better time to market than outsourcing is. As they say "post hoc, ergo propter hoc" or "after it therefore because of it". Something changed after we outsourced therefore it must be because we outsourced. It is always dangerous to jump to conclusions without proper analysis.

Time to market has been a key consideration for National Rail Enquiries. They don't need to be completely cutting edge, but they can't allow their customers to get too far ahead of them in the products they wish to use, and so a quick time to market is essential to keep up with customer needs. Outsourcing gives National Rail Enquiries access to expertise that speeds up the product life cycle but their level of involvement in the process helps ensure direction is maintained.

Defining the Requirements and Understanding Your Business Better

Just the process of going to tender for services can concentrate the attention on what is required to do the work and forces a review of what is being done, and whether it is done well, can be done better or needs to be done at all (Morse 2013b).

Very often a service being delivered in-house can run on for years without a review of what it is delivering and whether it is offering best value for money. You can review the service without going through a tendering process but the decision to outsource is often the catalyst for a thorough look at what the business needs from a service, and this can very often deliver service improvements outside of the specific service being outsourced.

This has been seen in the outsourcing of prison services in the UK. The first contracts were let in 1992 and private companies now run around ten per cent of the prisons in England and Wales. The competitive process that has been undertaken in this outsourcing has given the overall prison service an insight into the costs of running the service and the desired outcomes. This has led to efficiencies across the service, not just from the outsourced parts of it.

Choice of Supplier

Picking the right supplier is a key factor in whether outsourcing will be successful or not. This is such an obvious factor that you can safely say most people would put it down as one, whether they are experienced in the industry or not.

When looking at suitable factors such as financial stability, technical competence, understanding of requirements, track record, resources, etc., these are similar in most tenders, but there are some that are worthy of special mention when considered in the context of complex outsourcing arrangements.

I would pick out the four main areas as being: fully measuring the in-house option, limitations in the economic assessment of the supplier bids, contracting in sufficient detail, and setting up adequate systems to monitor supplier performance (Willcocks, Fitzgerald and Lacity 1996). I will expand on these, and some others, below.

a)   Evaluating supplier bids against the in-house option is always going to be difficult. Whilst this may at first seem part of the "outsource/ don't outsource" decision, it is really a choice of supplier. There are likely to be a number of supplier options as well as the in-house option, but evaluating the latter can be problematic, as different costing methods may apply, and working out the cost of the in-house option may not be straightforward.

b)   Identifying the full costs of the in-house option needs to look at not only what costs can be saved but also what cost-saving opportunities will exist (Willcocks, Fitzgerald and Lacity 1996). For example you may have a manager of two functions, outsourcing one function may mean that you still need the manager but, whilst the cost isn't saved immediately, it does create the future potential for saving the cost depending on what happens to the other half of the role. It also may realize a benefit from the manager having more time to spend on the other function. Also, identifying in-house costs depends on the cost allocation methods used internally, the cost of change (including one-off costs such as redundancy), the timescale of the costs (how long term do you look forward to compare against an outsourced option) and the level of confidence in the current cost base (for example, could savings be generated by reorganising the in-house option or just by changing the way things are done?).

c)   Other issues with the in-house option are the impact of different service-level agreements (SLAs) that may be demanded of a supplier and how those SLAs, and indeed the supplier bids, are benchmarked against the in-house option.

d)   However, the main considerations in comparing the in-house
        option are very often the political ones. There can be internal
        pressure both to maintain the in-house option and to outsource.
        Maintaining the in-house option can be pushed for reasons of
        PR (don't want to be seen to get rid of existing staff), personal
        empires (outsourcing may mean a loss of control), job security
        (it may be your role being outsourced) or just a distrust of
        outsourcing in principle. Pressures to outsource may include
        the idea that change will be easier once a service is run by a
        third party. Sometimes you know what needs to change in the
        in-house operation but it is just easier to outsource it to someone
        who will make those changes rather than try to drive through
        the changes yourself. Sometimes the push to outsource makes
        positive investor PR by being seen to cut direct headcount and to
        be seen to be taking action.

e)   When evaluating the financial proposal of the supplier bids
        the client should always check for the balance of flexibility and
        control. The balance between being able to change costs as the
        service develops and being able to enjoy a fixed rate has to be
        to the satisfaction of the client. The desire to get a fixed price
        to give certainty should be tempered by the developments
        that may come during the term of the agreement (for example
        technological advances may help reduce costs in a more flexible
        arrangement) and also by an understanding of the risk margin.
        Fixed price puts risk on the supplier which they will charge for.
        The client needs to understand what risk it is placing on the
        supplier and whether it is worth the money (the allocation of
        risk is discussed later in the book, most notably in Chapter 7,
        but also in Chapters 8 and 9, contrasting the approach to risk in
        different sourcing models). There is a constant trade-off between
        flexibility and control (Quinn and Hilmer 1994).

f)   There is also a need to show a full understanding of requirements
        and full costings in the proposals. Too often an attractive price can
        turn out not to be so, due to hidden costs. These can arise because
        of poor contractual terms, poorly defined requirements, failure to
        allow flexibility for future changes and not allowing the supplier
        a reasonable profit.

g) It needs to be ensured that the supplier has a full understanding of the requirements and that these are documented in the contract. Whilst outsourcing needs flexibility for future changes, the current requirements should be fully understood and documented (Levins 1996; Law 1999).

h) The client bears some responsibility for this. Whilst the rule of "caveat emptor" may apply you really don't want a supplier putting in a low bid because they haven't understood the requirements. It can only lead to strife throughout the term of the agreement.

i) The service monitoring systems should be fully understood and should reflect the needs of the client. There is a danger in setting these to achieve short-term savings whilst longer-term efficiencies are sacrificed. We all want immediate benefits but thought should be given to the longer term. The performance monitoring regime should be geared to both the client's short and long term requirements and should reflect the benefit to the client over the term of the agreement rather than just the immediate impact (Law 1999; Langfield-Smith and Smith 2003).

j) As well as financial flexibility there is also a need for flexibility in the provision of the services. Many businesses are fast moving in a fast-moving world and there should be confidence that the supplier is going to develop along with the client and the business sector. There cannot be many things worse than signing up for a long-term agreement with a best-in-class supplier who becomes mediocre part way through the term of that agreement (Levins 1996). Technical flexibility is also a benefit and has rated highly in studies (Saunders, Gebelt and Hu 1997).

k) This requirement for service flexibility brings in the tender evaluation criteria of, what we called at National Rail Enquiries, "like, trust, believe". An outsourcing contract is usually a lot more than a supplier delivering a service to SLAs for a price. The world is often more complex than that, and outsourcing suppliers need to be offering innovation to their clients the ability to work well with other outsourcing suppliers who may well be competitors of theirs. "Successful relationship management requires more than a service provider delivering on SLAs" (Buffo 2004).

The whole area of relationship management will be addressed later, but at this stage I am raising the issue of a "partnership" arrangement as part of the supplier selection. Can you work with them?

The choice of supplier goes through the stages of supplier experience, understanding requirements, financial stability, the supplier's attitude to risk/reward systems, supplier independence and how you feel about them (Levins 1996). If at any of these stages you are not happy about the supplier you should consider eliminating them from the process. If you can't find a suitable vendor then maybe the in-house option is the one you want. Don't exclude the "do nothing" option.

Approach to Outsourcing

Deciding on the specification and requirements, choosing the supplier and getting the supplier to clearly understand those requirements and needs are essential to successful outsourcing (Zhu, Hsu and Lillie 2001; Claver, Gonzalez, Gasco and Llopis 2002; PA Consulting 2003a; PA Consulting 2003b).

However, deciding what to outsource and why and whether to go with one supplier or many is also part of the decision process prior to implementing a long-term outsourcing strategy (or not implementing one, as the case may be) (McIvor 2000; Costa 2001; Whittington 2001).

The client needs to decide to outsource based on sound business reasons and as part of an overall strategy. Following the flow may not be a good reason to outsource (Loh and Venkatramen 1992) although it is one that does come up (Bhattachaya, Behara and Gundersen 2003). It can often be a response to the hype and publicity surrounding the subject (Willcocks, Lacity and Fitzgerald 1995) and can be followed because others are doing it. You can ask the question "is following the flow a bad thing?". On its own as a reason, probably yes, but if others in your industry have been successful with outsourcing then there may be no good reason why you shouldn't. Outsourcing can be good short-term investor PR and an outsourcing strategy can improve investor confidence, which in itself is a good thing provided the strategy can deliver. There have been cases of stock prices increasing because a company has decided to outsource. The markets have seen this as a positive thing even before any benefit has been seen.

Much of the latter part of this book focuses on the approach to outsourcing so I have only briefly touched on this here.

Exit Strategy

Strange to say but a key part of any outsourcing strategy is the exit. The issue of the exit needs to be considered at the beginning as part of the overall agreement. It may not help the service run well but, if it has problems, greatly eases the transition to another contract.

Exit strategy has implications for both client and supplier. Many years ago there was an article in the *Financial Times* (Timmins 2004) about the handover of the £4 billion UK Inland Revenue systems from Electronic Data Systems (EDS) to CGEY (Cap Gemini) and how EDS realised that whilst "it might be on the losing side this time, it might be on the winning side next time". EDS wanted to have "a reputation for being professional going in, and professional going out". It reminds me of the approach of Gardner Merchant when they lost a contract and were in the run down process to hand over the service to the incoming supplier. Always do your best at the end, it leaves the door open to getting back in again and makes it difficult for the incoming supplier to make a noticeable improvement. Once you have lost a contract the best outcome for a supplier is to leave on good terms and have the incoming supplier seen to be doing a worse job.

A clear exit plan helps both the client and the supplier and should be included in the contract. However it does need to be kept up to date throughout the term of the agreement. The service changes as time passes and to assist in maintaining that service in its current form and to help the supplier understand what is required of them the exit plan needs to be kept current.

Strategic Focus

Again I will only cover this briefly at this stage as it is covered in more detail later in the book.

Many writers talk about the advantages of outsourcing allowing you to "concentrate on your core business" (Currie and Willcocks 1998; Lankford and Parsa 1999; Costa 2001), but the phrase "core business" is becoming less clear as business develops and indeed will change as the markets and the client businesses evolve. What may be considered core to your business now may not be so in a few years' time.

Strategic outsourcing allows companies to lower their long-term capital investment and leverage their key competencies as many companies, including such illustrious names as Apple and Nike, have done (Quinn and Hilmer 1994). Sun Microsystems concentrate on hardware and software and outsource just about everything else (Drtina 1994). National Rail Enquiries, my recent employer, outsource just about everything and see their core competency as understanding the customer's needs and being able to procure and manage services to meet those needs.

In the oil industry I saw that the big oil companies outsource much of their supply chain, with companies such as Schlumberger providing services for seismic survey, data analysis for reservoir optimisation, the supply of drilling equipment and the testing of the wells. The recent gulf oil spill that has caused so much pain for BP has brought to the attention of the public the fact that BP weren't the company sealing the well. That was outsourced to Halliburton, and also the rig wasn't 100 per cent BP owned. In the oil industry even the petrol stations are often franchise operations and are not directly owned by the oil companies.

Strategic focus is more important than the individual decisions on what to outsource and what not to, as it guides all those individual decisions. As a broad principle for outsourcing, a firm should concentrate only on those core activities that enhance its unique marketplace advantages (Drtina 1994).

Outsourcing can be started as incremental where it starts small to overcome problems or shortfall in expertise. It can be started where the company has either drifted into it or been pressured into it without a clear idea as to the objectives.

However the most successful outsourcing usually comes from a strategy to outsource for sound business reasons (Agar 2003).

As far as strategic focus is concerned, the strategic goals of the organisation need to be understood by the staff involved in establishing an outsourcing agreement, in order that those goals can be successfully incorporated and embodied (Embleton and Wright 1998). You can't expect strategic focus if the people involved do not know what the strategic goals are.

The research (Willcocks, Fitzgerald and Feeny 1995) has shown three paths into outsourcing:

1.   Incremental where the client starts small in discrete areas to overcome shortfalls either in expertise or cost.

2.   Hard learning where the approach has been to drift or be pressured

into outsourcing without experience or a clear idea as to objectives.

3.   Strategic where the approach is based on how it fits best with the rest of the business and how it can be managed.

Not surprisingly, the third approach has been shown to be the most successful but many client organisations are in outsourcing through the first or second route.

The outsourcing framework in Chapter 10 concentrates heavily on the need to keep the outsourcing strategy aligned with the overall strategy of the client organisation. Outsourcing should be seen in the light of the overall strategy and should support that strategy rather than being an afterthought.

Competitive Advantage

As part of an overall strategy outsourcing may be able to give a client organisation competitive advantage. "Outsourcing is a powerful strategic lever, which if effectively utilised by senior management can significantly differentiate the host organisation from its competitors" (Kakabadse and Kakabadse 2003).

This may be through factors of cost, time to market, new technology or many other factors. The point is that there are experts out there who can help improve your business without feeling the need to compete with you. It can help as a differentiator from competitors.

An alternative view to this is the one that questions whether supplier staff will be as motivated to discover competitive advantage as internal staff (Gantz 1994). I would counter this by saying that the business is still yours. Outsourcing can help you to gain competitive advantage, but never assume that the supplier will deliver this for you.

It is difficult to argue that the financial success of outsourcing is not a demonstration of the value it has to client organisations and that its continuing success suggests it is more than just a cost reduction strategy.

Third-Party Dependency

One of the most repeated arguments against outsourcing is that it makes you dependent on third parties who may not share your aims and objectives

(Levins 1996; ICAEW 2001; Kern and Willcocks 2002). The ICAEW paper raises many questions on third-party dependency "you lose the important advantage of having people on site who answer only to you". Becoming too reliant on one supplier can indeed be a risk, but this is partly mitigated by your choice of supplier. Choosing the best fit supplier with the right attitude and cultural fit to supply a large part of your outsourced services may be a lower risk than picking a poorly fitting supplier for a small part.

Multi-sourcing can help mitigate the risk as you can never be completely sure about your choice of supplier. Breaking up the service into smaller chunks limits the exposure to a poor supplier and the competition this can create between suppliers can help motivate them to a higher level of performance. An analysis of 62 outsourcing decisions in 40 organisations shows that as the outsourcing competition increases clients have "more power to bargain for shorter contracts, more selective services and better financial packages" (Lacity, Willcocks and Feeny 1996).

This is not to say that the downside of third-party dependency does not exist or can be fully mitigated. The best outsourcing company in the world does not necessarily have the same objectives as their clients (whatever their sales pitch may say) and this is a problem that has to be recognised. The outsourcer is there to make a profit for themselves. That objective may put them in line with the clients, as far as a long-term relationship is concerned, but then again it may not.

Even with multi-sourcing the risk does not go away. You are still likely to lose internal expertise and this increases your reliance on the supplier and makes you more dependent on them.

As with many business decisions, especially in outsourcing, there is a downside, in this case the increase in dependency on third parties. The trick is to assess if this is a bad thing and, if so, to see whether the advantages outweigh the disadvantages.

Quality

Outsourcing can improve the quality of the service for reasons already discussed (concentrated expertise, a higher level of technical investment, economies of scale leading to greater investment in training and staff development, etc.) (Hill 2000; Claver, Gonzalez, Gasco and Llopis 2002). As well as having an immediate impact this also is a strategic differentiator.

Quality can be a differentiator between a company and its competitors and strategic outsourcing decisions recognise this and focus the outsourcing in areas that can make a difference.

Flexibility

A successful outsourcing contract needs to reflect the long-term requirements of the parties and so should be designed to accommodate the flexibility needed to survive and react positively in the given industry (Claver, Gonzalez, Gasco and Llopis 2002; PA Consulting 2003a; Raynor and Littman 2003).

I have already touched on the advantages of flexibility, and the strategic value of this cannot be overestimated. Seagate Technology is a case in point. Seagate relied on in-house production and struggled when markets required more innovation whilst its competitors, who relied on outside suppliers, succeeded (Drtina 1994).

The contractual terms are key in getting flexibility; an outsourcing contract should have the required level of flexibility built in without making it weak. Service-Level Agreements should describe services, not procedures, to give definition to the contract but not be too prescriptive on how the outcome is achieved. Outsourcing providers prefer the client to tell them what they want done rather than how to do it. That allows them to be more innovative in delivering the service and so helps them be more competitive in their bidding (and consequently better for the client).

It is a difficult balance to achieve as being prescriptive with the supplier increases control but reduces flexibility. How this balance works depends on the service being outsourced and the outlook of the client. One of the issues with public sector outsourcing, from my experience, is that they tend to be more inclined to describe exactly how the supplier should provide the service which limits some of the value of outsourcing.

Problem Solving

Outsourcing can sometimes be motivated by the desire to offload a problem area to those better suited to cope with the problems. However this may not be a good idea (McIvor 2000; Zhu, Hsu and Lillie 2001), if there are problems these may be due to fundamental issues that will not be resolved by handing them to someone else and indeed may get worse with the client losing a degree of control. As Michael Dell once said "companies that outsource often turn a problem they cannot manage into one they can manage even less".

Even if you do manage to offload a problem, if the supplier cannot fix it then they are likely to give it back when it can. Ultimately it is your business so it remains your problem, whether in-house or outsourced.

Summary

It is difficult to get your head around the "chicken and egg" situation in this section. The outsourcing strategy should be driven by your business strategy but, at the same time, a better understanding of the factors involved in outsourcing may impact on your business strategy.

As with any strategy it involves thought, wide involvement and some crystal ball work. We may not know what is around the corner but a flexible outsourcing strategy can help you cope with whatever is there.

Chapter 4
Financial Factors

Let's not kid ourselves. We can talk about quality of service, speed of change, being better able to meet customer needs, future flexibility etc., but much of outsourcing is financial, especially cost reduction.

This chapter explains the financial factors involved in outsourcing and covers how those cost reductions are achieved. It is always good to understand how things happen even if you may not see that as your responsibility.

However there is more than just cost reduction to the financial factors in outsourcing. It can have cash flow and balance sheet impacts and can also help with understanding the costs of various services as well as sometimes helping to bring cost causation in line with revenue – the latter being a useful way of smoothing out profit fluctuations.

However, having said all that, the first thing I will look at are the cost reduction factors.

Reduction of Costs by Economies of Scale

It makes sense that a specialist supplier can benefit from economies of scale and that these savings can, in part, be passed on to the client (Drtina 1994; McFarlan and Nolan 1995; Evans and Wurster 1997; Finlay and King 1999; Kakabadse and Kakabadse 2000; Heshmati 2003).

These economies of scale manifest themselves in a number of ways.

PURCHASING POWER

By aggregating the volumes of a number of clients, outsourcers can get better pricing through higher volume. This can be through raw materials, equipment, software, service supply, etc. Software, as an example, very often has a fee scale based on the number of users but the rate drops as numbers increase – so a single licence for one hundred users is very often cheaper than having ten lots of ten-user licences. Similarly, equipment bought in higher volume can not only attract volume discounts but also reduced delivery costs on a per unit basis. Very often a delivery will cost the same if it is for 10 units as if it is for 100 units so the cost per unit will drop.

The purchasing power can often be seen to be more important in specialised areas. Something like PCs most companies use, but specialist equipment such as high-end servers most companies will not use. Therefore the purchasing power of the outsourcer can be more marked as the client may not even require one server, only a part of one. In this case the savings can be more significant as an outsourcer with eight clients, each needing half of a server capacity and processing power, can buy four servers as opposed to the clients between them having to buy eight.

However with volume purchasing usually comes standardisation, and there are downsides to this (Fill and Visser 2000). As discussed earlier, outsourcing can lead to a common standard and not excellence, due to the "one size fits all" approach that outsourcers can sometimes use.

COST OF CAPITAL/LEVEL OF INVESTMENT

Another economy of scale can be seen in the cost of capital and the level of investment.

Outsourcers specialising in a certain area can benefit from specialist financing packages that recognise the unique nature of the investment being financed. This may not be possible for the client firm, as the level of financing they may require for the area that could be outsourced may not be high enough to attract these economies.

Also in this area I would include the benefits of the scale of investment possible for outsourcers. Going back to the IT world again, an outsourcer may be justified in buying more powerful servers to meet the needs of many clients. It isn't just the economy of scale from volume but also economy of scale from technology.

SPREADING THE OVERHEAD

The economies of scale that large companies benefit from in the area of overhead costs also apply to outsourcers.

As companies get bigger they are able to rationalise their overheads costs and get better use out of the overhead they have. For example a company may start with an FD but as it grows it doesn't need another one. One person on accounts payable can cope with a range of invoice volumes, and in the period from the bottom of that range to growing to the top the company benefits from economies of scale in its overhead costs.

This works for most companies but the difference with outsourcers is that the benefit doesn't come from the growth of one company but, because the outsourcer has other clients, from many. This growth is also concentrated in a limited area so the benefits are greater.

AFFORDING THE EXPERTS

The final economy of scale for outsourcers, which ultimately benefits customers, is the ability to afford specialist experts.

A good example of this is translation services. Because of their specialisation translation companies can afford to retain staff who are able to speak many languages to a high level of fluency both written and spoken. A UK company may not be able to afford to retain people on their books who speak Russian, Greek and Arabic (unless it is coincidence that someone in a permanent role can also speak those languages) for the rare occasions that they may need those language skills. However, a translation service working on many different languages for many clients can.

The whole issue of economies of scale is one of the areas to be considered in the decision of single-sourcing as opposed to multi-sourcing.

You can get greater economies of scale if you single-source as the volume you are giving the supplier is greater, but you do lose some of the advantages of multi-sourcing. I will go into more detail on the advantages of multi-sourcing as opposed to single-sourcing and other sourcing models later.

Reduction of Costs by Cost Arbitrage

The main area here is the outsourcing of services and functions currently fulfilled in a more expensive country to being fulfilled in a country where costs, especially labour costs, are lower. Current examples of this are the outsourcing by UK companies to other countries, such as India, of finance and admin, IT development including software coding, call centres, business processing and legal services. For companies operating in wealthier countries there is a smorgasbord of different options with different cost differences and different skills and social issues. Countries such as South Africa offer better language skills and a smaller time difference from Europe, but less of a cost saving when compared to somewhere like India or the Philippines.

This is a cost saving that is fairly straightforward to realise. A person answering calls in Newcastle will cost more than someone answering calls in Mumbai. As long as you get the issues of knowledge and language skills right there is no reason this shouldn't work and help you realise a significant cost saving.

National Rail Enquiries outsourced their call centres to a company operating in India many years ago and this has proved to be very successful. We took the view that we were going to reinvest some of the labour arbitrage in improving the quality of the service and this has resulted in an increase in customer satisfaction from the levels achieved when the calls were handled in the UK. Some of this may be due to the system improvements that we brought into the call centres with the assistance of the outsourcing company, and some may be due to the increased emphasis in training and product knowledge, but the end result is a significant reduction in costs and an increase in customer satisfaction. More importantly, National Rail Enquiries have seen a reduction in customer dissatisfaction (more importantly because high dissatisfaction is more likely to mean people travel less than high satisfaction is to encourage people to travel more).

However offshoring doesn't always go well and, even more than in onshore outsourcing arrangements, you need to make sure that the client and the supplier understand each other. The client needs to make sure that they know what is being delivered and the supplier needs to know what is expected of them. Misunderstandings are more likely when you are dealing with a company in a different country, especially one that may not have the same first language as you.

The advantages of offshoring have gone beyond the original contact centre contracts, with countries such as India now offering IT services including coding as well as business processes and legal processing. These contracts have historically worked better than the old contact centre agreements. This may be because these services have a greater perceived importance to the client, and so benefit from a greater level of resource and effort on the part of the client, or may be that with the passing of time people, both supplier and client, are getting a better understanding of the pitfalls of offshoring and are better able to avoid them. Whatever the reason, offshoring arrangements are improving.

Reduction of Cost by Efficiencies

Outsourcing is often seen as a way to improve efficiency and reduce costs across the business (Hurley and Schaumann 1997; PA Consulting 2003a; PA Consulting 2003b). This is one of the key drivers for outsourcing to get the benefit of outsourcing efficiency and cost reduction. However, the client needs to know how these efficiencies will be delivered and how they can encourage, and benefit from, these efficiencies.

The setting of service-level agreements (SLAs) is a common method of deriving greater efficiency from an outsourcing contract. These can be set to improve over time to give the client organisation a future improvement path. However there is a word of warning on SLAs in that they need to be relevant to the business and of use to that business. As David Otley said "what gets measured gets done", so if you set SLAs the supplier will concentrate on delivering those regardless of whether they are really to the clients benefit.

The client also needs to be sure that the SLAs are economically achievable. You don't want a supplier signing up to unrealistic SLAs and then having problems for the rest of the contract term as they can't achieve them.

SLAs need to be flexible to adapt for future changes to requirements: what is relevant to the client today may not be relevant in the future, and what is a useful efficiency when the contract is signed may not stay so. Businesses operate in a rapidly changing environment and need to ensure that the contracts they enter into also can change rapidly. Indeed inflexible service-level agreements can be a distinct disadvantage to the client as the supplier is working to achieve targets that are no longer needed and not working to achieve those that are.

For this reason it is difficult to rely on contract SLAs and this is where proactive relationship management shows its value, by allowing an ongoing discussion and level of understanding that preempts problems. Relying on contract terms risks creating confrontation which will help no one.

The modern approach to SLAs is more of a risk reward approach, where efficiency gains are shared by the client and supplier. This helps to avoid the redundancy of out of date SLAs and concentrates the supplier and the client on real efficiencies, rather than those that are perceived at the beginning of the agreement.

Apart from SLAs delivering ongoing efficiency improvement there are underlying reasons why outsourcers can supply services cheaper through efficiency. The efficiency of production, mostly relating to economies of scale, can help to reduce costs. Apart from economies of scale there is the concentration on one form of production that helps reduce costs through improved expertise. A system repeating the same process can get better improvements due to that very repetition.

As well as process efficiencies staff skills can improve efficiency in an outsourcer with a greater concentration of skill on particular tasks.

One other area where an outsourcing agreement can deliver cost savings can be the avoidance of future cost increases. For example, inflation can be contractually capped to help the supplier avoid adverse future fluctuations. This can also help protect from currency fluctuations by getting the supplier to do the work on hedging and/or take the currency risk.

The capping of inflation has worked well in areas where costs have changed dramatically over a short space of time – something like the sharp increases in IT salaries in the late 1980s and early 1990s is a specific example.

You could argue that these cost risks would be covered in the pricing by a competent supplier but it may also be that the supplier is in a better position to handle these costs than the client. Again a good example of where this may be the, previously mentioned, benefit of protection from currency fluctuations. The supplier may be handling many clients in different currencies and would therefore have the expertise, and the systems in place, to handle the risk better, as well as being able to offset or net different client risks.

However there isn't universal agreement that outsourcing suppliers are inherently more efficient and benefit from greater economies of scale. Some of the following counter-arguments are often cited.

- Mass production efficiencies have a diminishing return. Many in-house operations can already be working at a high volume and the benefits of going to a greater volume outsourcer are negligible. There is also more to production efficiency than volume, as some smaller operations can be run more efficiently than larger operations (Willcocks, Lacity and Fitzgerald 1995).

- Labour specialisation efficiencies are partly reduced by employment legislation (TUPE in the UK and in the EU Acquired Rights Directive) meaning that staff transfer over to the supplier, therefore the service can end up being run by the same people.

- Large suppliers use their staff across many contracts to help their efficiency and help give staff a career path. This means that the supplier expertise efficiency can be a little blunted by supplier staff being moved around from contract to contract so individual clients do not realise the full benefit.

Most modern outsourcing agreements have an approach more towards risk reward scenarios where efficiency gains are shared by client and supplier. This way there is motivation for both sides to see efficiencies realised and to work together to realise those efficiencies.

Management Costs

Putting a service out to an outsourcer isn't a "fire and forget" process. When considering cost reductions clients need to take into account the cost of managing the outsourcing relationship.

It is tempting to reduce this and rely on the supplier in order to maximise the benefit, but this can be counter-productive. As will be seen in later chapters reducing the effort in managing outsourcing relationships can end up costing more than it saves and this is a big contributor to outsourcing failures (Zhu, Hsu and Lillie 2001; PA Consulting 2003a). Even if you can remove a layer of management costs you may well find you need another level of management with a different skill set. "In order to extract maximum benefit from the outsourcing deal, the buyer must manage its deal with the supplier in a structured and co-ordinated way" (Law 1999). This links back to the previously discussed issue of control (Langfield-Smith and Smith 2003).

The outsourcing framework in Chapter 10 covers the important issue of governance and the resource that the client organisation has to put in to manage the outsourcing relationship. The smart thinking is that, whilst there may be a reduction in management costs from outsourcing, any reduction in the management overhead should be carefully considered and looked at in light of the new management requirements for running the supplier relationship.

My own experience at National Rail Enquiries has shown me the level of management that is required client side in any outsourcing relationship. If you want it to work you can't just leave it to the supplier and it isn't just a case of putting bodies on the job. The client needs to ensure that the management team is not just resourced up but also has the skill set to run an outsourcing operation. These skills may well be different from the skill set required to run an in-house operation.

Conversion of Fixed Costs into Variable Transaction Costs

This may seem like a minor benefit of outsourcing but converting an overhead or fixed type of cost into a variable is a benefit to some clients.

There are usually fixed costs in any operation but a specialist outsourcer can spread these, and volume risk, across a number of clients and operate on a variable cost basis. For example a call centre obviously has fixed costs (management, communications, parts of IT, rent etc.) but outsourcing suppliers can offer a straight cost per call price to clients.

In many cases variable costs are preferable as they can align activity and possibly revenue with costs. As activity goes up costs go up and whilst this may lead to higher costs, those costs are linked to activity and so likely to be linked to revenue, thereby reducing financial risk.

This charging mechanism is especially applicable if the client is concerned over productivity and has variable demand (Overby 2012). There is continuing development in IT outsourcing on charging mechanisms with cloud computing changing the hosting model to a "pay as you go" commodity type of service, where the pricing is transparent and you only pay for what you use. This has some obvious advantages over buying your own hardware and communications for your own server farm, especially if your demand for capacity is variable.

From my personal experience I would be wary about placing too much weight on this "advantage" of outsourcing except in circumstances where the conversion to variable costs is explained through the supplier's volumes such as it is in cloud computing arrangements. Converting a fixed cost into a variable charge places the risk with the supplier and, if this risk is out of their control, the risk margin they charge may be more than the benefit of the change in the cost profile.

Cash Flow and Balance Sheet

Outsourcing can have an immediate cash flow impact as the supplier may buy the assets it is taking over or they may take over capital purchases for the future (Law 1999; Hill 2000; Bhattachaya, Behara and Gundersen 2003). This can also have the effect of taking assets off the balance sheet improving performance indicators such as return on investment (ROI). This area is especially noticeable in public sector outsourcing, where the level of public borrowing is a key economic indicator. There is significant pressure in the public sector to use supplier funding (Morse 2013a).

As with the previous factor, on conversion of fixed costs into variable transaction costs, so can capital costs, and the cost of financing that capital, be converted into variable transaction costs allowing the client to vary costs with demand and activity (Verizon 2004; Corrall 2013).

This does clearly have a cost. The risk of investment recovery is passed to the supplier as is the cost of financing. Also the benefits to the client balance sheet by way of asset reduction will have the opposite effect on the supplier by increasing their asset base. All of this will need to be factored into the price.

Some of the cost factor in this depends on the relative cost of capital between client and supplier. If the supplier can benefit from a lower cost of capital it may be that the client can benefit, at least in part, from this lower cost. However, in some cases the position may be reversed and the client may have a lower cost of capital than the supplier. This means that you have to carefully consider where the cash flows lie so that the deal can be structured to deliver maximum efficiency.

Another factor to take into account is the exit strategy at the end of the contract. If the supplier owns the assets this can complicate the exit strategy and the client may face significant exit costs.

Risk Sharing

There is a logical argument that an outsourcing supplier is better able to mitigate risk than its clients as it has larger facilities and a number of different clients (Clemons, Reddi and Row 1993; Mathe and Perras 1994; Law 1999). Between the scale and the variation in clients there may be opportunities to reduce risk and, if the risk can't be reduced through scale, offset risks between different operations. For example one client may have a resourcing risk due to high volumes in the morning and low in the evening, creating the risk of either under- or over-resourcing. If another client has the risk of low volumes in the morning and high volumes in the evening the outsourcer with both these clients can have steady resource levels and offset the risks raised by the two clients.

However the client needs to ensure that the legal and commercial aspects of the agreement correctly allocate risk. If risk is unfairly loaded onto the client it takes away from the benefits of outsourcing but if the risk is unfairly allocated to the supplier it risks a higher price. The balance needs to be right and should reflect where control lies.

National Rail Enquiries recognised this in one of their early call centre contracts. They had an objective to reduce call volumes and migrate contacts to cheaper self-service channels. We have been very successful in this, taking call volumes from 100 per cent of our contacts just over 10 years ago to less than 0.75 per cent of them in 2013.

In an environment where call volumes are reducing there is a risk on the supplier if the price is a cost per call. The costs for setting up the operation need to be recovered and if this is factored into a cost per call then falling volumes create a risk of under-recovery. Similarly there is an element of fixed costs that are difficult to reduce quickly.

The solution National Rail Enquiries came to was to put aside the traditional cost per call model and split the costs into four. Set-up costs were to be charged as a fixed amount, either up front or monthly over the term of the contract (including financing charges in the latter option). This removed any risk of the supplier under-recovering the set-up costs and, from the client side, removed any risk of them over-recovering.

Fixed costs were based on forecast volumes and fixed for six-month periods. It was assumed that the supplier would be flexible enough to vary certain fixed costs such as desk space, training overhead, management levels, etc. if they were given enough notice and also given the protection of six-month periods where there would be no change to charges.

There was also a variable cost element which was a cost per call and was designed to place the risk of resourcing the people answering the calls correctly onto the supplier. This meant that the supplier was expected to take responsibility for the call handling time and daily and weekly variations in volumes. This is not unreasonable as they are the experts at running call centres.

Lastly was the risk reward matrix expressed as a percentage of costs (so the value of the bonus or penalty was linked to the size of the operation). Things such as customer satisfaction and, possibly more importantly, customer dissatisfaction were given targets and penalties and bonuses were built around under- and over-achievement. The same was set up around availability (which in call centres is measured through the percentage of calls that are answered out of those offered).

The aim of this cost model was to place risk where there was control of that risk or, if it was out of everyone's control, on the client. This last point is important as there are areas where risks really are out of the control of client and supplier. In the case of National Rail Enquiries this could be snow in the South East of England or an accident on some part of the network, either of which would send call volumes unexpectedly high. In this case National Rail Enquiries gave the supplier the benefit of "void" days, should call volumes be outside of a certain tolerance of forecast. The calls on these days would be paid for but excluded from the risk reward calculation. Whilst outsourced it is still your business and, if the risk is outside of the control of both the client and the supplier, then our default position is that the client should take the risk.

The issue of risk sharing also came up in my contract catering and facilities management work. The issue here was very much a balance of risk and control. If the client was prepared to let more of the control lie with us, the supplier, then we could assume more of the risk. This was especially true in large facilities management contracts. The more the client allowed us to take control of how things were done, the more we could absorb risk as we had more ability to offset those risks. We could see mutually exclusive risks and factor in the cost savings by way of reducing the risk margin.

The risk reward pricing model means that the client and supplier share the risk but also share the upside. It is more of a partnership pricing model and works best where the client is comfortable with the level of governance required to make a partnership work (Overby 2012). The client is sharing the upside and downside potential so needs to be more involved in the management of the contract.

Risk and reward is a bit of an overused phrase but to reflect the partnership nature of modern outsourcing relationships it is becoming more and more the reality.

Transparency

Getting an invoice for a service gives a great deal of transparency of the cost of that service. The invoice does not give you complete transparency, as there will still be internal costs to take into account such as supplier management, processing of transactions in the finance systems, cash flow impacts, etc., but it is still better than the internal costing option. Internal costings tend to rely on overhead allocation methodology which is difficult to get right from a practical point of view and nigh on impossible if there are internal political influences trying to influence or manipulate the presentation of internal costs. With an outsourced operation you get an invoice that includes nearly all the costs of the service.

However this transparency can take away some of the flexibility in the service. Very often a service will be outsourced and show savings but soon after the client realises that getting special changes now costs money when previously it was absorbed in the "fat" of the operation. In reality it brings about the realisation that the saving wasn't as much as was expected, as the opaque nature of the internal service costs hid additional services that were being provided free of charge. In an outsourced operation these additional services attract a charge, which can not only impact on the actual level of saving but can stifle experimentation. It is not so easy to get agreement to try new things when there is an invoice at the end of it.

You can argue that the in-house operation shouldn't have had "fat", but that ignores the reality of in-house operations. Much of the benefit of outsourcing is taking out that fat but it comes with the risk that the "fat" was really a slush fund for trying out innovative ideas or for absorbing the cost of one-off work.

My own view on this is that it is a risk but only if you blindly "bank" all the savings from outsourcing. If you realise that this is an issue and budget for additional costs for the flexibility of the supplier providing additional work then this shouldn't be a problem.

Another area of transparency that needs covering is the transparency of supplier costs. Many contracts are now being agreed on an open book basis so that, especially in the area of change control, there is some ability for the client to verify the costs. This will always be controversial and there are questions about the value of open book (for example, the ability of the client to judge the appropriateness of the costs) but in many cases it is a big step forward in outsourcing arrangements meaning that clients feel more comfortable with the relationship.

Summary

Cost reduction is one of the first things that leaps to most people's minds when outsourcing is mentioned, and let's not ignore the fact that it is an important factor. However it isn't the only factor and isn't even the only factor in the list of financial issues.

Whilst we all want to reduce costs it is important, as it is in other business decisions, not to ignore the wider picture when looking at the factors involved. It isn't all about getting things at a cheaper rate.

Chapter 5
Summary

I have covered the main headings of what outsourcers offer as opposed to the in-house options, those being technology, human, strategic and financial. However I hope I have also made it clear that it really isn't that straightforward. These areas can seem beneficial at first glance, and may well be beneficial at all future glances, but there are circumstances where the benefits may not be realised and may not even exist.

There are also areas where legislation makes some of the issues unavoidable. TUPE and the EU Acquired Rights Directive are unavoidable parts of UK and EU legislation and have a significant impact on the outsourcing industry.

The benefits of outsourcing are there but care needs to be taken in realising them and much of this depends on what you outsource.

What Do You Outsource?

The oft quoted statement that you don't outsource your core business has some logic to it but you need to answer the question as to what your core business is. This requires some analysis of what you do and, more importantly, what makes you successful. The things you do that make you different and successful are the core parts of your business rather than all of it.

It is important that the decision to outsource, and what you outsource, is part of a strategic plan relating to the overall business strategy (Willcocks, Fitzgerald and Feeny 1995). The research has shown three paths into outsourcing:

1. Incremental, where the client starts small in discrete areas to overcome shortfalls either in expertise or cost.

2. Hard learning, where the approach has been to drift or be pressured into outsourcing without experience or a clear idea as to objectives.

3.   Strategic, where the approach is based on how it fits best with the rest of the business and how it can be managed.

Not surprisingly the third approach has been shown to be the most successful but many client organisations are in outsourcing through the first or second route.

What is considered "core" even changes over time. Car manufacturers now, to a greater or lesser extent, do not directly manufacturer the parts, do not produce the marketing for the cars and do not handle all of the distribution and sales of the cars (Whittington 2001). This is true of Ford, as will be seen in the example later in this section.

Outsourcing a core part of your business could be the road to hell (Levins 1996) but, following the example of car manufacturers, what is core? (Kakabadse and Kakabadse 2003).

A simple example of this could be a company that makes cutlery. They regard making and selling cutlery as their core business but what is that? The process of the business involves excavating raw materials, shipping the raw materials, refining them into usable metals, designing cutlery, making the metals into the designed cutlery, shipping them to stores, marketing the cutlery and selling it. It also involves customer service, after sales, finance, commercial, legal, procurement, contractual and many other smaller functions to make it all work.

What is the core business? Is it all of these or just certain parts? They are all essential to the business so by some definitions are all core, but it is unlikely that any business would directly control all of these functions and are likely to use other businesses to provide part of the process.

The key to deciding what is core is to decide what makes your business successful and what you are good at. This is the core competencies question and it isn't an easy question to answer. It sometimes means you need to rethink what it is you do. However, this question is key to any successful outsourcing strategy as it ties your outsourcing strategy into your business strategy.

There obviously isn't a right or wrong answer to the question "what is core?" but a good way to start this analysis is to look at what others can do better. National Rail Enquiries arrived at their outsourcing strategy by looking at what others could do better than them.

Case Study: National Rail Enquiries – Provider of Travel Information to Rail Passengers in Mainland UK

National Rail Enquiries run a wide variety of back-office systems providing journey planning, fares and fares availability, real-time predictive systems taking up-to-date data and converting that to predicted train arrival and departure times as well as static data, for example station facilities. These systems need to be compliant with industry standards, need to be up to date and need to be maintained to technological standards and customer requirements.

National Rail Enquiries also provide multiple customer-facing channels including the website, SMS, mobile internet, call centre, mobile applications, speech recognition, TV apps and social media. These customer-facing channels are subject to extreme demand fluctuations that are largely unpredictable, such as bad weather and rail disruption. National Rail Enquiries also runs a large number of third-party services by way of B2B offerings.

Throughout all these services it needs the customer service, financial, legal, contractual, procurement and industry expertise to make them all work.

This type of business meant that National Rail Enquiries was faced with a number of issues:

- A wide variety of customer-facing channels.
- A fast-changing customer requirement for these channels. For example, mobile apps and social media are recent additions to the suite of channels and even those have a wider spread (mobile apps cover iPhone, iPad, Android, Windows, Blackberry, Palm etc.).
- A high level of risk in what new channels will succeed and become a significant contributor to customer needs.
- Highly complex industry systems (including a phenomenally complex fares system).
- A wide demographic for users (something like 65 per cent of the adult population in Britain use rail at least once a year, and in turn well over half of *these* use National Rail Enquiries).
- Customer requirement for a number of different systems (journey planning, real time, static, etc.) under one banner.

These wide and varied requirements together with the risk profiles led to a review of the outsourcing strategy which ended up with multi-sourcing. The path to that decision was long and iterative (we didn't come to it after a few days brainstorming in a locked room) but the results have been successful.

Firstly look at the customer-facing channels. This is information and not retailing so the ability to engage in many channels is, to a certain extent, easier. There are no credit card details to take, in fact no personal details at all so there is little data protection compliance required. The user interface can be made to be simple and tailored to deliver a specific range of information even taking in some personalisation, such as frequently used stations, to make the process easier.

However the simplicity of the customer requirements increases the expectation of the spread of channels. Certain demographics want to be able to talk to a person so call centres are needed. The reduction in call volumes over time brought in the need for an automated overflow in times of high volume, which is where the speech recognition system comes in. Many people use the web, and the move to mobile technology includes the need for mobile internet and mobile apps as well as SMS. However mobile isn't a single channel, what with Apple, Android, Palm, Blackberry and Windows operating systems, and then there are tablets, all of which display the mobile and standard websites differently, as well as requiring different apps.

The choice facing National Rail Enquiries was to employ a vast array of skills to meet all these channels or outsource to various expert organisations. In this situation it is an easy decision and National Rail Enquiries outsource the development and maintenance of all their customer-facing channels.

Similarly the back-office systems are diverse and complex. Journey planning on the GB rail network is very complex and when you add to this the millions of different fares you have a huge system with a large variety of different options and rules.

The real-time system has to take a number of different feeds (the National Rail Enquiries one takes 17) and handles millions of enquiries every day. It uses predictive and heuristic technology, not just to know what is happening now, but to predict what is going to happen in the near future and give the customers an idea of what times the trains will be running later on down the track.

There is also a lot of static data including station facilities and ticket types.

Given the variety of systems required and the volumes that need to be handled, both in volume of data and number of enquiries, National Rail Enquiries also decided to outsource their back-office systems.

These drivers, at both ends of the business, make outsourcing an obvious strategy but this strategy drives the type of outsourcing model we chose, which drives our approach to governance and that approach to governance drives our staffing structure and the type of people we employ.

Delving back into my past I can find another example to demonstrate how organisations approach the core or non-core conundrum.

Whilst I was working for Gardner Merchant, the catering company in South East Asia, we set up a joint venture with Serco to provide facilities management to defence organisations, especially in Australia.

We won a contract to supply facilities management to the Australian Army at an army base in Puckapunyal, Victoria. In the tender facilities management meant just about everything and this is an excellent example of the core or non-core decision, as the army decided that their core purpose was training and everything else could be outsourced.

We took on:

- Catering (hence the Gardner Merchant involvement);

- Cleaning;

- Laundry;

- Gardening;

- Running the dentist;

- Running the pharmacy;

- Running the cinema;

- Providing the lifeguards for the pool;

- Running the base fire brigade;

- Clearing ordinance from the tank firing range.

- Etc., etc.

For all these functions we had to take care of:

- Staff training;

- Supply of goods and services;

- Meeting various service levels and performance indicators, and;

- Taking much of the risk on variations (I recall part of the risk assessment process included an estimate as to how many fires we could expect in a year so that we could put a risk value to a high number of fires and the cost of the flame retardant foam that needed to be used).

Basically the army needed to turn up, drive the tanks to the range and fire the shells. We did everything else.

This wide level of functions and responsibilities may sound daunting at first but having this breadth of responsibility also allowed us to realise cost savings and other efficiencies. For example the swimming pool was open for a short period in the afternoon where a lifeguard was required, but the cinema was open in the evening. With multi-skilling we were able to get some of the work across the two services done by the same people. Similarly, the cleaning and laundry allowed for a certain amount of cost reduction by combining some of the staffing.

If the services had been tendered individually, or on a "body hire" basis rather than an output-based approach, we wouldn't have been able to realise the synergies and make the cost savings.

Another example of a company deciding what is core and what isn't (and in this case changing their minds over time) is the Ford Motor Company. In the 1920s shortage of raw materials stalled production at Ford so Henry

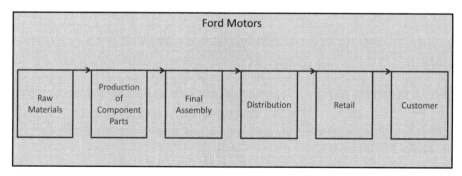

Figure 5.1   **Ford's Vertical Integration Model during the 1920s (Gash and Panchamia 2013)**

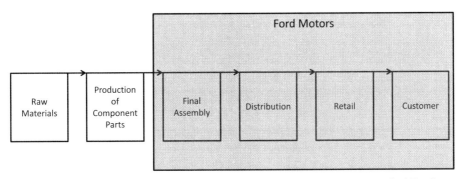

Figure 5.2   Ford's Supply Chain Model from the 1960s Onwards (Gash and Panchamia 2013)

Ford decided to own the supply chain. He bought steelworks, glassworks, timberlands, iron and coal mines, etc.

This was very successful but over time this became unfashionable and Ford outsourced much of their supply chain.

However there are always alternative views and some people are advocating a return to vertical integration in the current tough economic times.

General Motors has recently bought one of its parts manufacturers, Delphi, due to the bankruptcy of that company. It needed to secure the supply chain. In China steel manufacturers have been buying Australian mining companies to protect themselves against increases in the price of raw materials (Moving On Up 2009).

The decision on outsourcing is also covered in a paper published by the Institute for Government in the UK (Gash and Panchamia 2013). In this report they raise a number of issues:

1.   *Is it difficult to measure the value added by the provider?*

    If there aren't clear measures to see what value is being added then it makes the service difficult to price and makes SLAs to monitor performance difficult to agree.

2.   *Are service outcomes highly dependent on the performance of other services?*

Services that depend on others are difficult to incentivise and measure objectively. The situation can arise where poor performance by another service makes it impossible for the supplier to meet targets regardless of their performance. It can also be true that over-performance elsewhere can help suppliers meet targets when they haven't really done so under their own steam. All this makes contractual SLAs and incentives difficult to formulate and agree.

3.   *Does delivering the service require investment in highly specific assets?*

If it does require these specific assets (human, technological, infrastructure, specialism etc.) then firstly it makes the cost of contracting high. The supplier will require investment to meet the requirements which will be reflected in the price. It also gives the incumbent a significant advantage at retender meaning that the client may not get the best value.

4.   *Is the service characterised by high demand uncertainty?*

This type of service places a high degree of risk on the supplier that will be reflected in the price unless the client mitigates that risk for them (as National Rail Enquiries have done with their call centres through the pricing structure).

5.   *Is the service characterised by high policy uncertainty?*

If policy is likely to change impacting on a contractual relationship then there is the potential for high exit costs or change control costs for the client.

6.   *Is the service inherently governmental?*

Does the service involve key policy decisions, is it central to law and order capability or does it work with a duty to protect the public? If this is the case then an outsourcing contract may not work.

These issues do not say outsource or don't outsource. It is never that simple. However they should be taken into account when making the initial decision and later in this book we relook at these issues and the mitigation around them.

The whole debate on what to outsource is a complex one that varies from business to business and varies even more so from the outlook of the client.

Core or non-core isn't a simple decision and involves a consideration of the overall strategy of the organisation as well as the competencies and future plans. What may not look as a likely candidate for something to outsource now may be suited in the future and conversely something that fits into the company strategy to outsource now may not when future plans are taken into consideration.

National Rail Enquiries decided that its core function is to manage the overall delivery of services. We were comfortable outsourcing the delivery of these services but not comfortable with outsourcing the responsibility and control for delivery of the overall service, and we were also not comfortable with outsourcing our future strategy decisions.

Summary

Whatever you decide on the core or non-core debate, one of the most important things to keep in mind about outsourcing is that it is still your business. The customer doesn't care that you have another company running the service and they will hold you, and your brand, responsible for any shortcomings. As I have mentioned previously, outsourcing has been described as a *cost effective way to lose control of your business* (Skapinker 2003) or as Michael Dell once put it, "companies that outsource often turn a problem they cannot manage into one they can manage even less". However, this doesn't have to be the case. You can outsource and improve the standing of your business whilst delivering cost savings, increased flexibility and achieving a faster rate of change.

PART II
What Are the Problems with Outsourcing, Why Does it Sometimes Go Wrong and What Can You Do to Mitigate Risk?

Chapter 6
Case Studies

I think outsourcing is great – I wouldn't be doing the job I am if I didn't. However even I accept that it can go wrong and boy can it go wrong!

In this chapter I try to show some of the problems through examples and case studies. In the next I will step away from this and share personal views on specific areas of outsourcing, mainly from my own experience.

A 2005 Deloitte survey of 25 large companies showed that one quarter had brought functions back in-house as they felt they could do the work more successfully themselves and for a lower cost. 44 per cent said that outsourcing didn't save them money. Nearly half cited hidden costs as the most common problem. The study found that clients look to outsourcing to cut costs, simplify processes and give them expertise that they either don't have or can't afford in-house. In many cases they find the opposite happens with increased costs and increasing complexity and they also find that they need greater management skills to manage an outsourced operation (Deloitte Consulting 2005).

In a similar survey by *Information Week*, 45 per cent of those surveyed cited poor service and lack of flexibility as problems that had arisen after they had outsourced a service. In addition, 39 per cent mentioned that hidden costs that had not been foreseen at the tender stage and had created a negative impact on the outsourcing relationship (McDougall 2006).

Even with the resources of the US Government outsourcing can have problems. Following the problems with the launch of the new healthcare (Obamacare) website, the President was quoted as saying about IT in the public sector "We've spent billions of dollars … and it's still not working the way it should" (Davidsen 2013).

In the analysis in this section I will use some examples of outsourcing failures, and go through the reasons why these may have failed, and relate these to general problems with outsourcing.

The first example isn't specific to a contract but comes from a report published by the Institute for Government in the UK. It is titled *Making Public Service Markets Work* (Gash, Panchamia, Sims and Hotson 2013) and covers issues that have arisen through the growing trend of outsourcing government services. It is based on government outsourcing but the issues it raises, and the mitigation of those issues, apply equally well to private-sector outsourcing decisions and arrangements.

To give an introduction to this report I can do no better than quote the foreword from Peter Riddell, the Director of the Institute.

> *This report is one of the most important that the Institute for Government has produced. It highlights many of the confusions and problems produced by the big changes in how public services are provided over the last 30 years. The private and voluntary sectors are now very large suppliers of taxpayer funded programmes – for example in health, care for all ages, employment and probation. Meanwhile the public sector providers that remain must now often compete for the right to provide public services.*

There has been a huge change over the last 30 years in the way that public services are provided with successive governments seeking to reduce costs by outsourcing. This started in the 1980s with the competitive tendering of rubbish collection and street cleaning services. It now spreads throughout the public sector including healthcare, defence, education and prisons, areas that would previously have been seen as "core". A review in 2008 judged the UK public services industry to be the most developed in the world second in size only to the US (Julius 2008). In this report it calculates that it accounted for over six per cent of GDP, was worth £80 billion in revenue and employed over 1.2 million people.

At the date of the report it quotes that roughly £1 in every £3 that the government spends on public services goes to independent providers. 39 per cent of the running costs of the Department for Works and Pensions is now through outsourced contracts (Hodgson 2013) and there is a political drive behind this. The UK Prime Minister, David Cameron, has said "From now on, diversity is the default of our public services ... instead of having to justify why it makes sense to introduce competition ... as we are now doing with schools and in the NHS ... the state will have to justify why it makes sense to run a monopoly" (Cameron 2011).

This change has met with varying success and some very high-profile failures. Many of these failures have baffled those in the private sector. Much of the blame in the press falls on outsourcing however, from the outsourcers' side, much of the blame falls on the public sector and how they approach and run outsourcing contracts. In the private sector you can understand an IT project overrunning on cost; you can also understand an IT project failing. However, the private sector struggle to understand how both can happen at the same time. How can the costs overrun when the project hasn't been delivered? Why are you paying for anything at all? The important factor of the role of governance still remains and market mechanisms need controlling (Gash and Roos 2012).

The Institute for Government report recognises a number of areas where problems occur.

Failure to understand the nature of the services being provided is recognised as a weakness. There are inherent difficulties in some of the services to be provided and the report found a lack of a systematic approach to dealing with these difficulties. It also highlights uncertainty about whose job it is to perform essential market oversight functions. In addition a lack of clarity has existed about whose responsibility it was to address problems. Responsibilities often lay in the wrong areas or lacked impartiality.

The final underlying problem was that there was a low capability in central and local commissioning bodies. Government is still developing the skill set to design and steward systems that rely on third-party providers. Outsourcing involves a much more open and iterative approach to engagement with providers but the government hadn't developed the systems to meet these requirements. `

The government is taking steps to address these issues but the report feels that it doesn't recognise the scale of the challenges.

The report makes a number of recommendations that are aimed at public-sector outsourcing but do highlight problems across outsourcing, and these recommendations should be taken on board by everyone in the industry, even if only to confirm in your own mind that you already have the issues in hand. Whilst market stewardship may be beyond many private-sector companies, keeping this in mind is important for long-term success and in larger organisations and in specialist areas it is very important, for example in oilfield service outsourcing for oil companies where there isn't a huge number of potential suppliers. Whilst it is a public-sector report the issues aren't unique to the public sector.

Recommendation 1:
Clarify Roles, Responsibilities and Accountability Arrangements

There is a need to clarify the roles that must be performed, who must perform them and how the organisations and individuals involved should be held to account for performance.

a)   Government departments should adapt and adopt the "market stewardship framework" (see Figure 6.1) to help work towards effective choice and effective competition.

This helps clarify roles and responsibilities. It moves from the desired outcomes to ensure choice and competition in the market. This is mainly relevant to government outsourcing but can also apply to large organisations that need to have some degree of control over the outsourcing supplier market. As a long-term goal these organisations need to ensure choice and competition in the outsourcing market as much as governments do. It is not in their interests to reduce the number of potential suppliers or discourage new entrants.

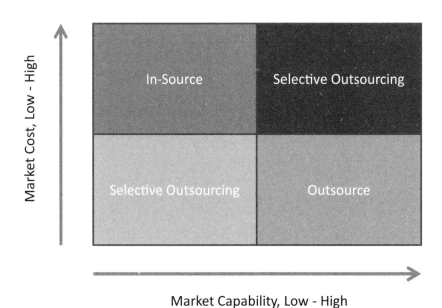

Figure 6.1   Market Stewardship Framework

Notes: * Assessed against democratically determined goals (e.g. quality, economy, equity). ** Inputs might include assuring access to a professionally accredited workforce, infrastructure, etc.

The second recommendation under this heading is to produce "accountability maps".

> b)   Accountability maps detail organisations and individuals responsible for each aspect of the market stewardship (as detailed in the previous section). This encourages a better understanding of the overall market performance rather than concentrating on individual supplier's performance. It takes the "market stewardship framework" to another level of detail.

The final recommendation under this heading is for better cross-department leadership.

> c)   This recommendation applies equally to private companies as it does to the public sector. Many companies are guilty of approaching outsourcing in a piecemeal way; overall leadership of outsourcing strategy will help in mitigating risk and in giving a complete knowledge of potential synergies. I have seen myself client organisations having individual departments pursuing outsourcing in their own silos and failing to realise potential cost savings and risk mitigation benefits that are there for a more holistic approach.

Recommendation 2:
Be More Considered, Open and Flexible in Design

> a)   Policy-makers and commissioners must systematically evaluate and manage the risks of contracting out services.

>> This starts from an understanding of the different risk profiles of outsourcing different services. From this you can foresee problems and put measures in to mitigate these risks. With a more strategic view and cross-department knowledge you can sometimes mitigate risk through combining services. When Gardner Merchant won the contract for the full facilities management of the Puckapunyal army base in Australia, the fact that we were fulfilling most of the services allowed us to reduce the risk profile of the individual components. The ability to move staff from different functions and plan services out so that they weren't happening at the same time gave us the ability to not only reduce the costs but also reduce the risk. This risk mitigation consequently benefited the client.

b) Commissioners should test supplier incentive systems.

Testing incentive systems requires people who understand the service provision from the supplier perspective. Effective incentive schemes need to understand the risk profile and where risk is controlled. The commissioners also need to understand the commercial model of the supplier as well as the output requirements for the client. Poorly thought through incentive schemes can not only not achieve the right outcomes but also encourage the wrong outcomes. Suppliers will largely follow the schemes set by the client, if those incentive or penalty schemes are excessive the supplier will build that into its pricing. The supplier will also price for risks that it believes are outside of its control and that may lead to financial penalties on the supplier. In the same way the supplier will not see much benefit on incentive schemes that have incentive payments that are out of their control.

The whole issue of incentive schemes is covered later in this book, but suffice to say that they need to be put together carefully and with a full understanding of everyone's commercial models and the operation of the service.

c) Commissioners should find ways of increasing flexibility.

The section on multi-sourcing demonstrates the flexibility of this approach but flexibility should be a goal for all outsourcing strategies. The report mentions the performance related break clauses in the new Work Programme but the issue of flexibility also covers the change control process (contracts rarely stay the same over their entire life), exit provisions, IP ownership, etc.

d) Monitor the value added by providers.

This is important for not just demonstrating the value of the agreement but also to inform long-term plans and monitor the effectiveness of incentive schemes. These will help the client to improve the outsourcing strategy in the future.

Recommendation 3:
Focus on Competition, Market Structure and Market Dynamics

This again concentrates on the long-term viability of the supplier market. If the number of providers goes down and new suppliers, with possibly new innovative ideas and approaches, cannot enter the market then the client will ultimately suffer. This may seem like something that is exclusively for the public sector, and that private-sector companies do not have the buying power to concern themselves with market structure, but this is not the case. Some private-sector clients are huge organisations and many operate in specialists markets where supplier numbers are already limited. Maintaining competition in the market is essential for the private-sector client as well as the public sector.

a) The client should conduct or commission regular market studies.

> Market studies should look at barriers to entry, barriers to expansion, any impact of competitive incentives, risk of provider contraction and provider exit.

> This market study should look to ensure that there are possibilities for small and medium enterprises to enter the market to avoid possible stagnation.

> This is taken seriously and when Her Majesty's Revenue and Customs were considering a new system of childcare vouchers they brought in the Office of Fair Trading to advise on market design.

b) External scrutiny should be encouraged.

> In the report it was recommended oversight by the Office of Fair Trading or the National Audit Office to maintain external scrutiny.

> In private companies there is a need for external (possibly being different parts of the same company) oversight of the procurement process and market design. It is easy to get comfortable dealing with a limited number of suppliers and there is a need to break away from that if it occurs. Again this isn't something that is specific to the public sector.

Recommendation 4: Increase Transparency

The Government have published details of upcoming government contracts to encourage a wider market response but the report recommends more.

It suggests providers of public service should:

- Publish details of the funding they receive from government.

- Publish their performance against contractual obligations.

- Publish the suppliers to whom they subcontract services, the value of these and, where possible, their performance against the contractual obligations.

It also suggests the rules on what is "commercially confidential" should be clarified for freedom of information requests. This will help transparency and help understanding of the agreements.

The report included case studies, which I will cover in some detail as they show the developments in public-sector outsourcing and show how successful those developments have been and indeed where they haven't succeeded.

CASE STUDY 1: THE WORK PROGRAMME (GASH, PANCHAMIA, SIMS AND HOTSON 2013)

The Work Programme was an initiative launched by the Coalition Government in June 2011 to help the long-term unemployed into work.

The Government had been commissioning services in this area for 20 years, but the results tended to be long-term unemployed returning to short-term work only to return to benefits.

The issues with the old system included:

- Payment of high upfront fees regardless of actual outcomes. This did not encourage a results-based approach.

- The incentives for placing the harder-to-place claimants were insufficient.

- There was little scope for services designed around individual needs.

- Suppliers were allowed to remain in the market regardless of results.

The Work Programme changed this by:

- Paying providers largely by outcome and sustainment fees.

- Paying higher rates for those deemed harder to help into employment. The differential fees were designed to compensate for the additional work for placing the harder claimants.

- Adopting a "black box" approach, allowing suppliers to design their own ways to achieve results.

- Shifting market share to higher performing providers.

This last change was something that National Rail Enquiries introduced into their call centre outsourcing contracts back when the volumes were still significant. We had multiple providers and the split of the calls was based on past performance. If you did well then you got more calls and so more contract value giving an additional incentive for suppliers to deliver top performance.

The Work Programme faces some inherent difficulties.

- It is difficult to measure how much of the outcome is due to supplier effort and skill and so it is difficult to measure the value added. A supplier could place someone in long-term employment because of the their own skill, effort and innovation, or it could be because of the efforts of the claimant, an improvement in the overall economy or some other factor. This may mean that suppliers are being overpaid with incentivised fees when the outcome is not due to them.

- It is also true that suppliers may be underpaid because poor performance is due to external factors and they fail to meet targets despite their good efforts and skill.

- This service is also subject to demand uncertainty. The number of claimants is largely dependent on the local economy. Low volumes and high volumes both cause issues for the suppliers, low volumes threaten their revenue and recovery of their investment but high volumes, especially if they are short term, give them the problem of ramping up a service without the assurance of an ongoing revenue stream at the higher level.

- The outcomes from the supplier's efforts are not solely under their control, it also depends on the performance of the local Jobcentre Plus and any training organisation the claimant is referred to.

At the date of the Institute for Government report (July 2013, i.e. two years into the initiative) the Work Programme was seen to be highly successful in some respects. It was implemented in less than 12 months and reduced government expenditure on outsourced employment services. The previous scheme cost around £1,600 for each referral, which has dropped to £1,200 under the Work Programme and is due to drop to £900 in the near future.

The new initiative has also helped cross-department collaboration, it now takes in former offenders who are referred to the Work Programme on the first day of their release.

However the outcomes from the initiative have been disappointing. All 18 providers have missed the target of getting 5.5 per cent of claimants into sustainable employment (the average performance was 3.6 per cent). Performance in other areas has also been disappointing, with some evidence that easy-to-help claimants have been given more help despite the differential payment regime. Furthermore, despite the black box approach, there has been little evidence of innovation and the new financial model has seen some suppliers leave the market due to the severe financial strain that this has introduced.

A number of reasons have been cited for these failures:

- Some see a need for improvement in the contract design.

- The payment mechanism and reliance on inaccurate forecasts may have discouraged supplier investment.

- The payment categories for various levels of claimant didn't work. There were nine payment categories, but suppliers felt these were too broad to properly categorise the different levels of challenge that were involved. Also the differences in value between the payment categories was not wide enough to reflect the level of cost for some groups making it difficult to justify the work on the harder-to-help categories.

- Financing (partially the lack of upfront fees) and regulatory arrangements were seen as creating barriers to market participation.

- The reduction in costs for the Government stretched the financial viability of the contracts.

- Performance management was seen as indecisive. The contracts did not allow for termination of the contract or the reallocation of market share in the first two years. This gave the Government very little in the way of hard penalties during this period. However, whilst there were few penalties for poor performance, some suppliers have commented that the reporting of performance was overly onerous.

- The "black box" approach to the methodology and processes the suppliers employ meant the Government took a light touch to issues with subcontractors, since they did not have visibility of the commercial structures. This meant that subcontractors were put into a difficult position, where they were suffering financially under the contracts. This was further exacerbated by the confidentiality clauses in the contracts between the prime suppliers and their subcontractors.

- The strict adherence to procurement rules may have meant that the best suppliers were not selected. The Government kept to strict EU procurement guidelines which they believed meant they could not take into account past experience. This led to some of the contracts being awarded to providers who had no track record in the area. For example, nine out of ten providers with existing contracts in pre-existing schemes won at least one contract in a geographical area where they had not previously delivered services, whilst five out of ten lost contracts in areas where they did have previous experience. This unnecessarily increased the time to ramp up in the new area and increased the transition costs as they needed to hire new staff, find offices, set up suppliers, etc.

- In addition there was a decision to relocate some providers to new geographical locations, risking the issues over setting up again and restarting relationships with Jobcentre Plus and suppliers.

- One of the issues that the report highlights as contributing to the problems has been high-level leadership, in that the high-level involvement was personal and senior. This meant that there were problems when personnel changed, as happened when there was a cabinet reshuffle and Chris Grayling was replaced as Minister for Employment, along with some other changes at senior level in the government. Also the seniority of the leadership led to departments pushing too fast and undermined the risk processes that may have helped avoid some of the issues. Usually the department trialled new initiatives but, because of the short timescales involved, this was not done in this case. Further to this, officials at the department wanted a phased approach to verify pricing, but this was also not possible with the short timescales. The short timescale reduced the time between the contract-award and go-live dates, which also impacted on suppliers who were starting in areas where they had not previously had experience as their ramp up was much steeper.

This case study, whilst admittedly having its successes, does highlight a number of areas of failure that are common in many outsourcing agreements that do not go as well as they should.

a) Taking the time to fully understand what you are outsourcing and how best to move into the new arrangement. In the case study above the lack of time was driven by a political agenda but this is an issue that impacts on many outsourcing decisions. Once businesses have decided to do something they naturally want to do it quickly and frustration will set in if it isn't going fast enough. This increases the risk of problems and, as has been seen with the Work Programme, the results can then be sub-optimal.

b) By trying to make the contract costs transactional the government introduced a level of complexity that made the financial model difficult for the suppliers and meant that it did not achieve the desired outcomes. A much more collaborative approach on the pricing structure would have helped mutual understanding and this issue may have been avoided.

c)   A blind following of procurement rules meant that real advantages were missed. Sometimes this is inevitable for the public sector as there are laws as to how it can proceed. However this is a lesson for private companies commissioning services, blindly following a procurement process in order to get the best deal may not work. Try to be flexible.

d)   There was a poor approach to change management by the department in this case. If they had a better change control process then, when issues first started to come up, the contracts could have been varied through this process. It is always a good idea to have a solid change control process in place. There will always be changes and amending the contract is usually easier than going through the whole tender process again.

CASE STUDY 2: CARE FOR OLDER PEOPLE (GASH, PANCHAMIA, SIMS AND HOTSON 2013)

There is an established market in care for older people with the privately funded care sector accounting for 50 per cent of provision. Even the publicly funded care is very often provided by outsource companies; between 1992 and 2010 the number of places provided directly by local authorities fell by over 70 per cent.

In the UK in 2013 this market was worth around £23 billion, the majority of which (around two thirds) is spent in a residential setting. The majority of the funding for this market (also around two thirds) is publicly funded.

The market itself is highly diverse with 90 per cent of providers only having one or two homes. The top ten providers provide less than a quarter of beds. (Blatchford and Gash 2012). This diversity of suppliers is one of the main strengths of the market.

However, this area also has a number of fundamental challenges.

- Value added is difficult to evaluate. It is difficult to assess, in a quantifiable way, the quality of service between two different providers.

- Added to this is the budgetary pressure that has led to the government forcing prices down, with a knock-on effect on quality.

- The budgetary constraints also put barriers in the way of funding for individuals, limiting choice and restricting the market.

- Choice for the consumer is difficult with limited information for a decision that, very often, needs to be made quickly. The Care Quality Commission (www.cqc.org.uk) does help in this area but they are chiefly there to highlight poor care rather than rate higher quality. The Care Quality Commission works on this basis because it is difficult to compare the quality of care therefore an approach to rate basic requirements, such as patient involvement in their own care and security of medicine storage, is effective in highlighting areas of concern. To try to rate higher level quality such as individual engagement and long-term mental stimulation is, at best, difficult and/or requires long-term assessment. The fact remains that much of the choice is placed onto the end user, or their families, when information about the choices is limited. This lack of informed choice leads to providers having less incentive to improve quality as the market for consumers is not working with consumers having full knowledge.

- There is often poor coordination between local authority departments leading to problems with care needs and avoidable additional costs due to higher administration to make the process work. My own personal experience, with my mother moving into a care home, strongly suggests it is an area where, through the lack of coordination in local authority departments, it seems no one is in charge. The decisions of end users and their families are not well informed and providers are therefore not measured on a fully informed basis. This could allow providers to "play the system" and gain a better commercial benefit than their performance would normally deserve. An imperfect market and/or process is not conducive to an effective service.

The following chart (Figure 6.2) from the report shows these issues graphically.

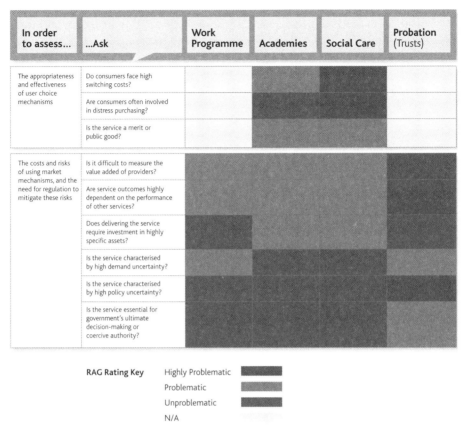

RAG Rating Key   Highly Problematic

Problematic

Unproblematic

N/A

Figure 6.2   Assessment of Outsourcing Decision

The funding issue is an area that makes this service especially difficult to manage. Not only are local authorities trying to keep rates down, the overall "market" for the services is growing. From 2005 the number of people over 85 has risen from 900,000 to 1.2 million. This is expected to double again over the next 20 years. A realistic view of the costs of the service needs to be ascertained so that the control of costs is realistic and does not unfairly impact on the service and the service providers.

This focus on cost impacts on the procurement process, with quality issues being considered secondary to cost. There is also some evidence of a lack of engagement and the local authorities adopting a more arms-length approach. These two factors together lead to an unimaginative approach to the tender process to the detriment of the end result.

This process leads to poor communication between departments, and poor care for the consumer, leading, ultimately, to higher costs as it encourages short-term fixes.

The report on this case study makes recommendations that show a close correlation with issues in the private sector:

- Clarity on roles and responsibilities. In this case the funding responsibilities are unclear, which leads to confusion and delay in decision making.

- Better information. This relates directly to private-sector areas where the measurement of performance can be difficult. In this case the lack of comparative quality measures makes it difficult for users to select a provider.

- Better coordination. A systematic approach to the issue is recommended. This will help both organisational coordination and budgetary coordination.

CASE STUDY 3: PROBATION SERVICE
(GASH, PANCHAMIA, SIMS AND HOTSON 2013)

The 2007 Offender Management Act 'set out new arrangements for the provision of probation services. The Act lifts from probation boards the statutory duty for making arrangements for probation services and places this duty on the Secretary of State who will contract with providers to deliver these services.

The Act enables the creation of new public sector bodies, probation trusts, with whom the Secretary of State may contract, alongside providers from the voluntary, charitable and private sectors'. (Community Justice Portal 2007)

This process has been developing for years but was stepped up in May 2013 with the Ministry of Justice announcing reform plans described as "Rehabilitation Revolution" aiming to open up 70 per cent of the probation service to competition by the autumn of 2014. The plan is to contract out the management of low- and medium-risk offenders and will pay providers both a fee for the service and a payment by results, the latter being measured in a reduction in re-offending rates.

The contracting out of probation services has received some bad press recently (Barrett 2013). This controversy has led to both Serco and G4S pulling out of some bids and some very harsh criticism coming from government including the withdrawal of some tenders that were progressing in the prison service. In November 2013 the Serious Fraud Office announced they were going to investigate both G4S and Serco over these contracts (Sourcing Focus 2013). That not only is a serious threat to the reputation and long-term financial standing of the businesses but it also cuts back their current bidding until investigations are concluded.

Whilst the suppliers claim they charged on the information they were given there has obviously been some serious problems with these contracts, regardless of where the fault lies.

The different probation trusts have different approaches to providing this service, with some entering into outsourcing in a small way whilst others enter into large formal tendering processes with national providers. However they follow three general principles similar to the decision to outsource in many organisations.

1.   What are the needs of the offender population?

2.   Are the services "core"?

3.   Do we have the expertise to deliver these services?

As with private-sector organisations and other public-sector departments, the probation trusts tend to keep core services in-house and outsource the non-core. They are also more willing to outsource when they believe that they do not have the expertise to deliver the services themselves.

However, as with most outsourcing decisions, the probation service faces a number of difficulties.

1.   The quality is difficult to measure. Whilst measuring re-offending rates is a proxy for quality it isn't a perfect measure. The link isn't straightforward and, as with many SLAs, there is the danger of suppliers working towards what is measured without a consideration of the long-term benefit. It has been seen that desistance from crime develops gradually so there is a danger that the SLA doesn't fit with the actual quality of the service.

2.   Suppliers are not alone in delivering the results. There are many other services that contribute to the SLA such as housing (getting people proper accommodation), employment (getting offenders into work) and health (getting proper treatment for offenders addicted to drugs and alcohol). The fact that the outcome isn't entirely in the supplier's control means that they could be rewarded, or penalised, for the performance of others. This is a common issue in outsourcing and a core issue with multi-sourcing (see Chapter 9).

3.   As we will cover in the chapter on multi-sourcing, when you have a number of suppliers (in this case both public and private) working towards the same outcome friction can develop which makes the process harder to manage.

4.   This type of service is relatively new so there isn't a huge market of experienced providers, with a track record of performance, to choose from. This increases the risk in provisioning the service.

The experience of the provisioning of these services has to date been mixed. There have been high barriers to entry leading to limited choice and fragmentation has meant that many contracts are uncoordinated.

The conclusion of the Institute for Government report is that there are a number of areas to focus on.

Yet again it focuses on roles and responsibilities being clear. It states that "it is critical to place the commissioning function at the right geographical level". The set off between national contracts that may achieve economies of scale and a more coherent strategy, and local contracts, that are likely to be more responsive to local needs, is one that the report says needs to be considered. Indeed this is an issue for many outsourcing agreements spread over a wide geographical or functional range.

In the report it emphasises that the organisations commissioning the service need to develop close relationships with providers (a key requirement for many outsourcing arrangements but especially in a multi-sourcing environment). The close relationship doesn't take away the need for robust monitoring of performance but rather is complementary to it. Effective relationship management will help to develop better coordination and so the better integration of services. In a world where no one supplier is fully responsible for delivering the end outcome, integration and coordination is essential.

The probation service is an excellent example of the issues facing some more advanced outsourcing decisions. It has the issue of performance being hard to measure, interdependency between this service and others for the final outcome, the supplier market being relatively under-developed, a high risk of the overall strategy that drives this outsourcing being changed and also the added burden of high-profile issues with contracts in this area.

The Institute for Government concludes that there are requirements for the Government to:

- Build capabilities in new areas;

- Develop strategies to mitigate inherent risks;

- Align functions to support effective oversight;

- Re-engineer the commissioning and procurement process to place greater emphasis on ongoing learning and adaption, collaboration with providers and coordination with other services.

This report from the Institute for Government and the case studies detailed above show some of the areas where outsourcing can go wrong and where the pitfalls can be avoided. These very much apply to the private sector. The public sector is a good source of this information due to the openness of the processes and outcomes. In the private sector much of the above report would have been kept internal and covered by confidentiality clauses. It would be a mistake to take the openness of the public sector as a sign that the public sector has a level of failure that is not reflected in the private sector. It is likely that this is only an impression caused by the level of publicity that public-sector problems attract and the amount of information in the public domain on these problems.

The UK National Audit Office has also produced a number of reports on outsourcing in the public sector, notably reports on managing suppliers (Morse 2013a) and the supplier's role (Morse 2013b).

In the first report, entitled *Managing Government Suppliers* and published on 12 November 2013, the authors look at the market and the steps being taken by the government of the time to improve the public-sector approach to outsourcing.

This report concentrates on what are known as the "strategic suppliers". These suppliers account for £10 billion in 2013 out of a total central government spend with third parties of £40 billion. However the report also highlights the £840 million that it estimates has been saved with these strategic suppliers in the 2012–13 year. Much of this saving has been generated by the central oversight that was introduced in 2010, mostly run by the Cabinet Office. Before these changes in 2010 there wasn't a central oversight of government suppliers, which is key in understanding the outsourcing relationship. Public and private sector alike need to see the outsourcing relationship in a holistic way.

The changes made by the Cabinet Office introduced reporting across departments for the 40 suppliers it had identified as strategic suppliers to the government. This included the amount of spend and reporting on performance against KPIs. It put in place Crown Representatives to manage a number of strategic suppliers across government departments.

These changes were not just bureaucracy. They generated real savings with an estimated £806 million saved in 2010–11, £437 million in 2011–12 and £840 million in 2012–13 (Morse 2013a). This is over £2 billion in three years.

Much of this has come from an approach to these strategic suppliers and the success of that approach has been helped by an understanding of how much is spent with these suppliers across the government. Prior to this work there was no complete record of how much was being spent with each supplier across the departments.

Large suppliers work across the government. For example, Serco have contracts with the Department for Culture, Media and Sport managing national sports centres. They also work with the Ministry of Justice on prisoner escorting and custody services.

G4S run admin support and marketing services for Visit England in the Department for Culture, Media and Sport and also run Her Majesty's Prison Birmingham for the Ministry of Justice.

Sodexho run Her Majesty's Prison Bronzefield for the Ministry of Justice and provide accommodation services for the Ministry of Defence.

Capita, Serco and Atos all have contracts with the Department for Transport and the Department for Work and Pensions.

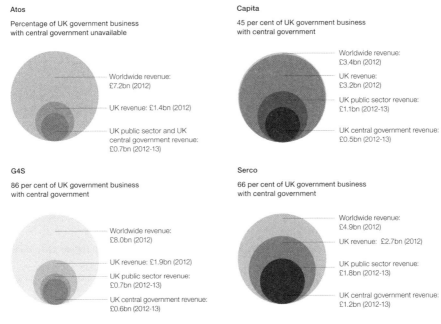

Atos

Percentage of UK government business with central government unavailable

Worldwide revenue: £7.2bn (2012)

UK revenue: £1.4bn (2012)

UK public sector and UK central government revenue: £0.7bn (2012-13)

Capita

45 per cent of UK government business with central government

Worldwide revenue: £3.4bn (2012)

UK revenue: £3.2bn (2012)

UK public sector revenue: £1.1bn (2012-13)

UK central government revenue: £0.5bn (2012-13)

G4S

86 per cent of UK government business with central government

Worldwide revenue: £8.0bn (2012)

UK revenue: £1.9bn (2012)

UK public sector revenue: £0.7bn (2012-13)

UK central government revenue: £0.6bn (2012-13)

Serco

66 per cent of UK government business with central government

Worldwide revenue: £4.9bn (2012)

UK revenue: £2.7bn (2012)

UK public sector revenue: £1.8bn (2012-13)

UK central government revenue: £1.2bn (2012-13)

Notes

1   Worldwide and UK revenue figures as reported in contractors' 2012 accounts, UK public sector and UK central government revenue are amounts received in cash in 2012-13 as reported by the contractors to the Cabinet Office.

2   UK public sector figures exclude devolved spending in Scotland, Wales and Northern Ireland.

3   G4S's UK public sector and central government revenue figures exclude £142 million of revenue from contracts relating to the Olympics (before the settlement).

4   Examples from the accompanying memorandum, *The role of major contractors in the delivery of public services.*

Source: For public sector and central government revenue: Cabinet Office – quarterly data returns from strategic suppliers. For full details see Appendix Three and source for UK and worldwide revenue: Contractors' 2012 accounts

Figure 6.3   UK Government Strategic Suppliers Revenue Split (Morse 2013a)

Figure 6.3 shows the level of business that four large suppliers do with the government, and specifically central government, out of their total UK and Worldwide revenues.

This gives an idea of the size of the prize for a client such as the UK Government looking at its outsourcing on an overall basis. Forming a Commercial Relationships Board with the Crown Representatives involved has moved the government into a more "best practice" mode of handling outsourcing relationships, where suppliers are seen as strategic suppliers to the whole organisation. Contracts are done for individual services but there is now an overview of the whole process. There is more strategic supplier management and also strategic supplier performance management. Data is collected across contracts and supplier performance is measured not just against the individual contracts but also across all departments.

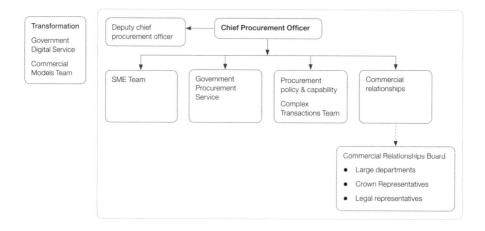

Figure 6.4   Cabinet Office Procurement Structure (Morse 2013a)

There is now an overarching structure and the position of Chief Procurement Officer as shown in Figure 6.4.

This role, the establishment of the Commercial Relationships Board and the introduction of experts from the private sector has also helped get the right skill set in place.

This structure follows similar processes to the best practice in Chapter 10. There is a role to:

- Agree and regularly review objectives and strategy;

- Set core priorities on managing suppliers;

- Agree and regularly review progress against planned work and planned savings;

- Monitor and support the resolution of risks and issues with suppliers;

- Make decisions on how to manage these strategic suppliers;

- Share significant issues relating to the suppliers.

With regard to the skill set in existing departments commercial skills gaps have been identified and put in as an improvement priority.

With this framework approach to outsourcing over £2 billion of savings have been made over three years. The approach isn't just theory, it does work.

The National Audit Office has also looked into four major suppliers to see whether they are delivering value. The four are Atos, G4S, Serco and Capita (the four shown earlier in Figure 6.3, on their UK Government revenues). These four suppliers provide a range of public services costing over £4 billion per year and the majority of this is with central government, with contract lengths varying from one year to 40 years.

This report entitled *The Role of Major Contractors in the Delivery of Public Services* looks at three main headings.

- Is there sufficient competition in contracted out public services?

- Can we see whether contractors' profits reflect a fair return?

- How can we know whether contractors are delivering?

On the first question on competition there is an obvious advantage in having more competition in the market. It increases innovation and usually helps keep prices down. However there are significant barriers to entry for new businesses where "the devil you know" can have an impact, especially in the more risk-averse clients such as the public sector. Large suppliers provide financial stability, they can absorb risk, provide investment and bring in economies of scale.

This preference for larger suppliers can be seen in the areas where there are large public-sector services. Whilst there are 200,000 suppliers to the government there are only three providers of private prisons, two providers of child custody and two providers of medical assessments. The seven services mentioned are split between five suppliers being Serco, G4S, Capita, Atos and Sodexho.

This arrangement has come in for criticism in the press especially in light of the Serious Fraud Office investigation of G4S and Serco. This has, possibly unjustly, been described as cronyism (Birrell 2013). Regardless of what is said it can be argued that so much business going through a small number of suppliers, whilst limiting some of the financial risk of dealing with smaller organisations and reducing management overhead, has its own risks. Having your suppliers investigated by the Serious Fraud Office for suspected overcharging can't be good.

To try to encourage competition the government have an aspiration to have 25 per cent of its spend on goods and services to go to Small and Medium Enterprises (SMEs). Unfortunately this aspiration includes SMEs providing services through larger prime contractors. Very often this puts financial pressure on the SMEs as the larger organisations seek to improve their margins and the ongoing process of larger organisations buying smaller ones can sometimes negate the benefit of this as the SMEs involved get bought by larger organisations.

The second question the National Audit Office asked is on contractors' profits. This is normally a small part of the cost and is there to cover the risk, investment and innovation that outsourcers can provide. Outsourcers very often run on small margins and can do this because of the risk profile they take on and because they can spread the risk across many clients. The outsourced providers of passenger train services in the UK run on around 3 per cent profit which is well below FTSE 100 averages (which ranges from 3 per cent to 12 per cent).

The level of profit doesn't appear to be a significant issue with outsourcing arrangements but there is the underlying feeling sometimes that these organisations are making money out of previously in-house operations. This can sometimes raise theoretical questions on the value of these arrangements but, the view of some unions aside, it seems clear that the other benefits outweigh the additional cost of outsourcer profit margins.

On the last question on whether contractors are delivering, the National Audit Office highlighted that some standards are difficult to describe as a service level in a contract. Government expect public services to deliver the services with honesty, impartiality, openness, accountability, fairness, integrity, transparency, objectivity and reliability. They expect this to be done within the spirit of the law, in the public interests, to high ethical standards and achieving value for money. All fine for an organisation's aspirations but difficult to word in a contract and even more difficult to define for service levels and performance standards.

The report highlighted that because of these difficulties the government needed to go beyond the measurable outputs and look at the outsourcers' governance and its management and control environments.

There have been a number of high-profile issues with services being provided on behalf of the government by outsourcers. Not the least being the involvement of the Serious Fraud Office in an investigation of Serco and G4S in regard to possible overcharging of costs for the monitoring of tagged prisoners. There are a number of other ongoing and concluded investigations into outsourcing contracts that will help the National Audit Office understand the issues and improve future agreements. This is likely to include improvements in corporate governance for the suppliers and a greater level of compliance monitoring by the various clients. After the issues that G4S had with security for the 2012 London Olympics, where Army personnel had to be brought in because G4S were under-resourced to fulfil the contract, they had an external review by PwC and have made internal changes to strengthen their corporate governance.

The report also highlights poorly calibrated KPIs as an issue. If these are set either too easy or too hard they can work against contracts being delivered well. It also realises the limitations of KPIs in that they are normally focused on things that are easily measurable.

To develop and add to the themes from the Institute for Government reports, I will attempt to add to that some more from my own experience and from discussions I have had with other outsourcing professionals over the years in the next chapter.

Chapter 7
My View

In the previous chapter we looked at case studies and examples but here I want to look at the factors that I believe can cause outsourcing to have problems and even fail.

They are in no particular order, and the weight of each one will depend on the situation, not least the importance of the service being outsourced. However as a whole I hope they offer some useful pointers.

Make Sure You Understand that This is a Relationship. While it May Not Be for Life, it Also Isn't Just for One Night

The National Outsourcing Association in the UK produce some useful guides, one of them being *Why Outsourcing Relationships Fail and How to Make them Prosper* (National Outsourcing Association 2013b).

This guide bears out some of the key lessons from my experience. Yes, an outsourcing agreement is a commercial and financial transaction, but it is also a relationship between people. Much like a marriage there is a need for soft skills to make it work and, without wanting to turn this into a marriage guidance book, there are a few points that may sound familiar to many of us.

- Communication is key. An open-door policy is a much overused phrase but it really means something and is relevant to outsourcing relationships. Miscommunication leads to a lack of empathy, lack of trust and a drifting apart of goals. Like a marriage it can seem easy but underneath there is a lot of hard work that goes into making it a success.

- Build the trust up through communication. This may mean formal communication processes being built in but there needs to be trust built up and maintained. Remember that trust isn't just confidence that the service will be delivered as per the agreement. It goes much further than that and reflects a willingness to help the partnership.

- Part of the outsourcing relationship can be as simple as delivering the goods. I say simple, but this involves both sides working together. The supplier has to deliver the service at the expected cost and also any other expected benefits such as innovation. The client needs to be there to enable the supplier to deliver.

- You need to have confidence in each other. As in any relationship confidence needs to be earned and is easily destroyed, but without it success will be an uphill battle.

- Avoid complacency (taking the other side for granted). The service and relationship will need to be constantly evolving and the danger of getting stuck in a rut is real. The business environment is constantly evolving so change should be business as usual.

- Avoid negativity and face-saving. Just as in managing staff, managing suppliers needs a positive attitude and the ability to make people or suppliers feel valued.

- Bring issues to the fore. Don't try to ignore them hoping they will go away; they might, but if they don't time is likely to make them worse.

- Be flexible. If you are going to dig your heels in make really sure it is for a reason that is worthwhile. Don't do it just to save face.

- Go the extra mile. Maybe not flowers and chocolates but a willingness to step outside of the contractual relationship will help build trust and help the long-term relationship.

- Avoid the memes. Organisations fulfil a basic tribal need for people but in outsourcing relationships the memes of that "tribe" can erode trust and create a combative atmosphere. Try to overcome this natural instinct and "unite the tribes".

The Life Cycle sourcing framework in Chapter 10 goes into more detail on suggested governance approaches. It details building up and maintaining the relationship and the processes for overall governance of an outsourcing agreement. This framework will help get the relationship set up right and keep it running right.

Make Sure You Understand the Costs of What is Being Outsourced and What You are Buying In

When you are comparing the costs of different outsourcing providers and, indeed the in-house option, make sure you are comparing apples with apples. If you aren't you need to adjust your assessment of the pricing to take into account offers that give you more.

If in doubt benchmarking, especially that performed by an outsider, can be useful in making sure that the costs for services are comparable.

Understanding this area sounds easy but when you get into detailed tenders, and especially trying to compare these to in-house costs, it is rarely simple. One of the issues is that it is highly unlikely that all the service offerings will be of the same quality. "Cost should always be assessed within the context of delivery quality or, put another way, as a component of the price/performance ratio" (Anand 2013).

The in-house option is especially difficult to cost. Internal accounting policies are often decided for reasons other than complete accuracy (convenience, political allocation of costs etc.) and getting an accurate cost for the in-house option is essential for any outsourcing decision.

Sometimes an external consultant is the best option, as they can look at the costs with a clear view and no internal baggage.

Make Sure You Understand What is Being Outsourced

Picking up from an article by Ephraim Schwartz in *InfoWorld* in 2008 we can demonstrate the importance of this point with the $4 billion deal between the US Navy and EDS.

EDS won the contract back in 2003 with a deal to manage voice, video, networking, training and desktops for 350,000 Navy and Marine Corp users. But after just one year EDS had to write off nearly $350 million because it couldn't get close to fulfilling the obligations it had under the agreement.

Whilst EDS take the responsibility for not fully understanding what was required when they bid, the Navy take part of the blame. With no one in the Navy taking overall responsibility for the project EDS had no one to go to for a definitive answer.

Marine Corps Lt Gen Edward Hanlon Jr called the project "rocky and problematic". EDS even had to delay the release of quarterly earnings reports because the projects finances were so muddled.

This failure can largely be put down to poor communication by the client and the supplier bidding without full understanding from the supplier. However I suspect that in reality the Navy may not have had a full understanding themselves.

The Navy also treated this as a service contract in spite of a huge hardware component. Col Robert Baker said "this was not an acquisition programme, but it required acquisition rigour".

One of the lessons that the Navy say they have learned from this project is to use a number of suppliers or multi-source. They do it for competition between suppliers (Schwartz 2008) and in Chapter 9 I will go over some of the other advantages of this approach.

It is also important to understand what is being outsourced, as leaving gaps in the outsourcing contract (which can easily happen if you don't have a full understanding of what is being outsourced) gives suppliers ample opportunity to inflate fees once they have the contract. This is not to say that suppliers will deliberately take advantage of a poorly prepared client, but they will bid for what you ask them to bid for. If you don't know what you want them to do then you run the risk of a poor deal and ultimately the rule of *caveat emptor* is likely to prevail.

Work for Success but Prepare for Failure

However well you think it is going, or going to go, you need to prepare for failure as part of the need for continuation of service.

The Institute for Government published a paper entitled *Commissioning for Success: How to Avoid the Pitfalls of Open Public Services* (Blatchford and Gash 2012), based on a series of workshops, that raised the example of the collapse of Southern Cross Care Homes where government was caught out by the financial failure of a care home provider and didn't have adequate contingency in place.

Often a way of preparing for this is making sure that the service is portable. In IT outsourcing arrangements this may mean the client owning Intellectual Property (IP) or at least having IP rights should the supplier fail. It may also involve the use of open source or non-proprietary software to ensure a quick and easy "lift and shift" of the service should a supplier fail.

The development of commodity hosting such a cloud helps in this area as it is now easy to shift software from one hosting environment to another provided the software is written to be able to do so.

This approach of portability of service has other advantages, which I will cover more under multi-sourcing, but it is one of the best ways to have an insurance policy for failure by a supplier.

Also under the heading of preparation for failure is the timing. When do you decide that a failure is either imminent or has happened? Handling this properly means having early warning systems in place, an intervention plan and the contractual mechanisms and rights to exercise that intervention.

Planning for failure requires an understanding of the main types of failure, service failure and financial failure. The first being poor or missed delivery and required standards not being met. The latter covers a situation where the supplier is financially no longer able to meet the requirements. These types of failure can be linked but the failure planning in either case needs to be related to the importance of the service. How long can it be undelivered, if at all?

Early warning systems will involve a regular review of the financial health of the supplier and the market, monitoring the quality of service (a deterioration in this is often a precursor to other issues) and looking at how the supplier may be impacted by other factors, such as the failure of one of their clients. For these systems to be effective they need to work quickly and need to be actioned quickly if required.

One of the very early warning systems is the contract itself. Pushing a supplier into unreasonable service requirements or financial terms could in itself lead to a failure. Whilst as the client you want the best deal, you do not want to precipitate a failure that you will ultimately end up having to fix yourself.

There needs to be an intervention plan which will hopefully lead to the current supplier remaining in place. This plan needs to be flexible to take into account individual circumstances but also needs to be prepared. It isn't something you want to be throwing together at the last minute. Often such a plan involves contractual "step in" rights being agreed up front.

Planning ahead reduces panic and helps maintain service continuity, both of which are to the benefit of the client and the supplier. It also helps if the plan is communicated. Whilst it may be uncomfortable to discuss the prospect of supplier failure with the supplier it is in everyone's interest to ensure this is in place and understood. The plan will include the step in rights that the client has and the process around that. It is wise to look at the fact that the step in may not be permanent. There may be instances where the client steps into the agreement to get the supplier over a temporary difficulty (either financial or service related) but this does not signal the end of the contract and the service can be handed back when the temporary difficulty has gone away.

There then has to be a mechanism to implement the intervention plan, which needs to include trigger points and a contractual right to intervene. You want to avoid the situation where you believe failure is imminent but you don't have the right to intervene and have to wait for the collapse of the service to be able to step in. You also don't want the terms of the intervention to be part of a dispute at a time when the last thing you want to be doing is having ongoing arguments between client and supplier.

The timing of the trigger points needs careful consideration. Not too soon as to intervene unnecessarily but not too late so that it is too late to avoid service disruption.

Planning for failure is a difficult concept especially when everyone is so positive at the start of an agreement. However it should be looked at in the same light as the contract. No one would enter into an outsourcing arrangement without a contract but also no one ever wants to have to go back to the contract. Contracts and failure plans are sensible precautions that everyone hopes will never be used.

Suppliers Need to Understand the Scale of What They are Taking On

It is all too easy for a supplier to overestimate the savings that can be made when you are bidding for a contract.

Firstly you want to win. Many contracts are on cost and however accurate your costings are it is going to be slow progress building your business if everyone else bids lower. The temptation is there to underbid in the hope that it will all be right on the night.

Also there is usually some arrogance on how much better you can do the job than the in-house option. "We have to be better than them, we are the experts". "If we weren't better than them they wouldn't be going to tender".

There is a tendency, especially where the contract involves significant workforce numbers, to believe that you can reduce headcount just by taking the work on.

Atos have recently run into trouble in the UK after they took on the work capability assessments for the Department of Work and Pensions. Their work has been criticised in the media and in reports. This led to the Minister ordering a quality improvement plan for Atos, including retraining and re-evaluation of staff. The Department have brought in PricewaterhouseCoopers to provide independent advice and Atos have brought in a third party to assess the quality of their audit and make recommendations for improvement. Atos are also increasing the number of staff on the ground to try to get waiting times down and improve the system.

There is a substantial risk that suppliers underestimate what is required and that will lead to problems.

Seek as Much Transparency as You Can

This impacts on both sides of the table. The supplier needs to understand as much as possible about what the client needs and the client needs to understand what the supplier is bidding for. The more you understand the less likely the thing is going to go wrong later.

Transparency is also important in pricing. Getting as much detail as possible in the pricing helps the client to see where the supplier may have misunderstood the requirements or missed something out. It also helps for the future as requirements do change and the more transparency there is in pricing the easier it will be to agree price changes around different requirements.

You could say "tough" if one side didn't understand what they were signing up to, however outsourcing relationships can be long term and for key services. It really doesn't work to have one side thinking the other took advantage of their errors, however deserving the pain may seem. This isn't a game for putting one over on the buyer or the seller. We will leave that to the dodgy used car dealers.

Transparency in costs also helps to compare different outsourcing bids and also helps you to flex the costs to see the impact of changes to volumes and operational models.

Make Sure the Tender is Clear and that the Client Side Bid Assessment and Negotiation Team Fully Understands the Tender

On this one I am going to call in some of my own personal experience. Gardner Merchant bid for a catering and cleaning contract for an Australian Army base (not Puckapunyal, but note that as with EDS this is the armed forces – different country, same problem).

The pricing schedule in the tender required the catering to be on a price per person/per month basis. However it gave no further details on how that was to be calculated and this gave us a problem.

How many people was the multiple to be? Was it the total on base or the total eating the catering being supplied by the outsourcer? Even though this was a remote site the numbers weren't always the same as people were ill, order pizza from the local small town or just weren't hungry. It also didn't specify how the number of people was calculated as the numbers varied when army personnel cycled in and out. Was it the average, the minimum number or the maximum number?

We asked questions through formal and informal channels and were told the client would get back to us but they never did. With the submission deadline looming we took a punt at the average number of people on the base.

We won the contract but when we issued the first invoice our calculation was questioned by the Army. They felt it should be the minimum number that were there during the month but offered no explanation why that was the case. We argued back and forth and had several meetings and eventually they agreed a contract "variation" to accept our calculation.

Over some beers a few months later the true story came out. The Army had brought in a tender "expert" to write the tender document and that "expert" then left them once it was issued. When we started to ask questions during the tender process they realised they didn't know what the calculation was supposed to be either so they tried to ignore us and hoped it would come out all right in the end.

When the invoice for the first month came in it was more than they expected (actually due to the fact that there were more troops on base that month) and someone higher up the chain of command questioned the cost. They then looked at how to get the cost down and picked the calculation method that would yield the lowest cost, regardless of logic, to help get the cost down to what they had submitted in the business case. Eventually they realised there was no logic in their method of calculation using the lowest day's number of troops on site (it meant an entire month's catering was based on one Sunday when one detachment had left and another hadn't arrived because of transport delays) but only agreed to our calculation if it was described as a variation.

With the benefit of hindsight this problem arose because of a lack of control by the client during the tender process. They had outsourced part of the tender process to a third party and had not managed that third party. This lack of oversight meant that, when the contract for the outside expert ended, they did not fully understand what he had done and so couldn't respond to the questions from bidders.

Clients – Don't Aim for the Stars!

We would all like a better service when we issue a tender but remember that everything has a cost. Suppliers can give you high quality services, very short contracts, certainty of costs and protection from risk but it all comes at a cost. You may insist that a call centre is to be in your home country in the West, rather than in India or the Philippines – but if you do the cost will be higher. If you want 99.99 per cent availability instead of 99.9 per cent you can probably get it but it will cost. If you want 24/7 cover instead of 06:00 to 21:00 you probably can but, again, at a cost.

The more you ask a supplier to do, and the more risk you place on them, the more they will charge, and you also risk limiting your market of suppliers with a consequent limitation on your choice.

When you wish to increase quality levels or change the risk allocation make sure you know the value of that change to you, so that you can factor that benefit into your business case. It shouldn't come as a surprise that costs go up but you should be able to compare those costs to the benefit in a "value for money" assessment.

In other words, if you ask for a Rolls Royce when you only need a family sedan then don't be surprised at the bill.

Make Sure You Have the Systems to Properly Verify Charges – Both of You!

This follows on from the earlier example used with Gardner Merchant and the Australian Army but here I could also use the accusations levelled at G4S in 2013 about overcharging for the tagging of prisoners in the UK.

This is for some prisoners allowed out of jail on certain conditions, usually including curfews. A tag is attached to them that they cannot remove and they are tracked whilst out of jail to ensure they keep to the conditions of their freedom.

The justice secretary accused G4S of overcharging tens of millions of pounds by charging for the tracking of prisoners when some had died, although the majority of the issue appears to have been around when the offender was back in jail or had left the country.

G4S has hit back saying that they charged in line with the contract and have accused court and prison services of failing to give them the information to prevent bills stacking up. Under the contract they were obliged to continue the service until told not to do so.

It would appear from the outside looking in that neither organisation has been particularly organised or proactive. The Government should have had processes in place to inform G4S when offenders came off the service and they should also have had systems in place to verify lists of who should have been tracked with the lists that G4S were charging for.

On the other hand, it is difficult to see how G4S could not have known that some of the offenders no longer needed tracking, even if they hadn't received formal notice of the end of the curfew order.

However, it may be that G4S were in the same position that Gardner Merchant were in with our Army contract. They may have been seeking clarification on the workings of the agreement and hitting a brick wall.

Whatever the reason it seems that the billing mechanism may have been agreed but the systems weren't there to make it work properly.

Test What You are Outsourcing

Schwartz also quotes an example in the medical industry (Schwartz 2008) where existing software, working fine pre-outsourcing, caused problems when used by a large number of users over a wide geographic area. Eventually the software was changed, but it took six months to recover.

The obvious error here was a lack of testing. Transferring the operation to an outsourcer should have meant that the client would take on some of the responsibility for understanding the limitations of the existing software. Hindsight is a wonderful thing but the "will it work" question is one that should have been considered at an early stage.

Does the Supplier Have the Right Skill Set?

An example here is from Hewlett Packard who had a successful manufacturing relationship with a Taiwanese manufacturer. This outsourcing relationship was so successful at reducing costs they handed over the work of writing instruction manuals and marketing materials to the same supplier.

Unfortunately this wasn't a core skill of the manufacturer and a lack of English language skills made this worse. It didn't work out well.

The fault for this clearly lies with HP for just assuming that a successful relationship with an outsourcer means it would be successful in other areas (Schwartz 2008) but the supplier does bear some responsibility for accepting work it must have known it would struggle to deliver.

I will come back to multi-sourcing, but picking the best of breed for each service is one of the core benefits of that strategy and this example shows one of the shortfalls of single-sourcing, giving everything to one supplier.

Do You Have the Right Skill Set?

The report *Commissioning for Success* (Blatchford and Gash 2012) highlights commissioning skills as being key to success.

It looked at UK public services, and participants to a workshop contributing to the report felt that Whitehall lacked commercial skills to develop the market and was instead focused on securing a good price. It recognised that commissioning skills are different, and broader, than procurement skills. Procurement skills is something the government already had but commissioning services required commercial expertise such as programme management, project management, financial and contract management and working to assess user needs. It also requires ongoing relationship management. Commercial skills will also allow the client to look at things from a provider perspective and allow the client to understand the market.

The report also highlighted the need for internal skills on market design. This involves a realisation that the client has influence over the market (especially with the volume and buying power of the government) and should use that influence to achieve the greatest value. That isn't a case of using buying power to beat out the best price but is a more subtle view of maintaining a competitive and developing market through incentives, support and financial structures. The client only has partial influence on this but it is a skill set that will help.

Sometimes you may have to accept that you don't have the skills and need to buy them in (recruitment, secondment or consultancy). Whilst that may not be ideal it is better to face that reality before you start the commissioning process rather than after.

I will touch on internal skills later under how you procure and manage an outsourcing contract but the internal skills are just as key as the ones the supplier is required to demonstrate.

Ensure Good Communication is In Place

In the EDS agreement with the US Navy, referred to earlier, another issue that arose was communication both between outsourcer and client and within their respective organisations.

EDS had problems with their staff turning up at bases to do work only to be turned away because the Navy wasn't ready for them. This was a significant cause of cost overrun and inevitably a significant cause of friction.

You need to ensure proper communication channels are in place and a framework approach to outsourcing, as described later, can help deliver this.

Ensure there is a Realistic Treatment of Risk

It is tempting for a client to try to push all the risk onto the supplier. This can increase costs (the supplier is going to want to be paid for risk) but it can also lead to failure.

In 2011 Capita took on work clamping and confiscating vehicles that did not have road tax on behalf of the Driver and Vehicle Licensing Agency. Unfortunately it took it on under the model of being funded by clamping release charges and the disposal of confiscated vehicles. Unfortunately the volume of these fees was not as high as expected and the revenue fell short. After two years Capita had lost £9 million and the Agency terminated the agreement early rather than renegotiate (Morse 2013b).

I believe you place risk where it can be controlled and where it can't be controlled the default should be for the client to bear the risk. It is, after all, their service.

Have a Good Contract In Place

You can't rely solely on good governance and a good relationship between supplier and client. Most outsourcing professionals regard the contract and the governance as complimentary. Research has backed this up (Poppo and Zenger 2002).

To get a good contract in place will involve legal expertise but you will need legal expertise with experience in outsourcing to make sure you get the right clauses and content into the contract. You also need commercial and operational back up for the legal team to ensure the contract remains a usable business document and works for the service being supplied.

Avoid the Lawyers!

Having got a good outsourcing contract in place you want to try to avoid using it and especially not move too quickly to the confrontational step of involving lawyers in contract dispute discussions. If things start to go wrong the lawyers really are a last resort. Neither side wins publicity when a disagreement over a contract goes legal. Ultimately there may be a winner (as well as the lawyers) but you should exhaust all options before going to this.

In 2005 Sears walked away from a contract with Computer Sciences Corp (CSC). CSC sued for damages and the whole painful process went on. Ultimately a deal was brokered but only after a good deal of pain and bad publicity (McDougall 2006).

Contrast this to JP Morgan Chase pulling out of a deal with IBM in 2004. They worked together to exit the agreement and both organisations came out of it with credit (McDougall 2006).

Many articles on outsourcing hammer home the importance of a good contract (including this book). However an ideal contract is one you sign then put in a drawer never to read again. You need a good contract to protect you but with good management you shouldn't need it. It is like an insurance policy.

Also you should avoid using the contract as part of the ongoing relationship management. If you keep bringing up the contract the other side will as well and eventually someone is going to have to use it. Best to keep it in that drawer until all else fails.

Another reason to try to negotiate rather than go legal is continuity. Unless the relationship has become irreconcilably damaged, or the supplier is in financial difficulty, you should seek to negotiate problems as this avoids the impact on the service of a confrontational approach.

However much we try to keep it on a business-like level when a client is threatening legal action it is difficult to keep focused on delivering the best service. If you are being sued there seems little to lose in cutting back the service to try to generate as much profit as possible while you still have the contract. As long as you continue to meet your contractual obligations you tend to go for the short-term gain, as the damage is already done by the legal approach of your client.

If the client decides to exit a contract but wants to benefit from a reasonable level of service during the exit period, it should attempt the negotiated route rather than looking for a confrontational legal route.

Ultimately you may find you don't have to exit but can resolve your issues within the current framework. Both client and supplier benefit if the existing agreement can be amended to resolve any service issues.

The Client Still Owns the Service Regardless of Who Delivers it Behind the Scenes

One recurring feature of failing outsource agreements is the client not taking overall responsibility for the service. One example of this is the NHS in the UK.

The NHS has involved numerous suppliers to deliver systems but due to a lack of overall control many of the systems are incompatible. Professor Ross Anderson from the computer security group at the University of Cambridge said "I fear it will be the largest ever systems integration disaster". Vendors involved included Accenture, CSC, Fujitsu, Atos, Agfa and Tata Consultancy Services. At one point it was costing double the original forecast cost.

The client needs to step in and manage the issues as ultimately they are responsible for the service and they can't contract that out.

Don't Make the Same Mistake Twice

It is astonishing how often clients go from an outsourcing agreement that isn't working to another that won't work either (Martin 2012). To quote George Santayana "Those who cannot remember the past are condemned to repeat it".

Clients should not dismiss a failed outsourcing contract as being the supplier's fault. That may well be the case but don't assume so. If the problems were created wholly or in part by the client then retendering is likely to bring about the same result.

If you have had a failed outsourcing arrangement then, before you dive back into the outsourcing world again, sit back and objectively work out what went wrong. Try to see where you could have done better and, even if it was the suppliers fault, try to learn from what went wrong and take a better approach to outsourcing the next time around. Outsourcing offers a convenient blame hound in that you can always say that it didn't work because of the supplier but in reality that is very rarely the case. Even in the most clear-cut cases of supplier incompetence there is always some blame attached to the client as they picked the supplier, agreed the contract and managed the outsourcing relationship. Somewhere along that line there must be some blame residing with the client.

Accepting the errors you made, either in supplier selection, contractual SLAs, contract terms, implementation, project management, service management, etc. will help you do better next time.

If you think none of it was your fault you will take the same approach with the likelihood that you will get the same result: failure.

Don't Be Afraid to Accept that Outsourcing Just Isn't Appropriate for This Particular Service, or At Least Not Now

In line with the previous point about not making the same mistake twice the process of analysing what went wrong may well come up with the answer that this particular service just shouldn't have been outsourced or at least it may have been a good idea before but now needs to come in-house.

It may be that outsourcing was a mistake or that the landscape has changed and it is now no longer appropriate.

We had a good example of this at National Rail Enquiries. Originally, when the website started to become popular, we wanted to sell display ads to offset the cost. We didn't have the expertise to do this ourselves so outsourced this to an agency who specialised is selling ads for publishers.

Initially this worked well but as the site volume grew we started to have problems. Rates were dropping and, of more concern, the agency wasn't selling the full number of ad impressions and we were running our own internal ads to fill the space.

When we analysed this we could see why this was the case. The agency was on a small cut of the overall revenue so small deals weren't worth doing. Selling a couple of million ad impressions for a one-off promotion (say selling ads to promote a tourist promotion in Edinburgh) wasn't worth the effort for the agency. Also they were balancing effort to revenue for the whole site so low-rate network deals worked for the agency as, whilst the rate was lower, it involved little work for them. One person sitting in an office could generate hundreds of thousands of pounds of revenue, albeit at a low rate. The alternative was to have lots of sales staff knocking on the doors of the ad agencies for higher-value deals.

When we looked at alternatives we saw that large sites such as ourselves had an in-house ad operation and this meant that there were no ad sales agencies that could deal with our volume. Because of this we decided to bring this service in-house, with an ad sales person and someone to handle the technical issues with serving the ads.

Whilst this increased headcount and costs, the increase in revenue was well in excess of the increase in costs. Even with an outsourcing-based organisation such as National Rail Enquiries sometimes we decide that some things are better off handled internally.

Another report from the Institute for Government *When to Contract* (Gash and Panchamia 2013) looks at the ease of contracting and how certain factors can make it more difficult to enter into an external contract. The report is for government contracting but many of the points relate to the private sector as well. In the report they raise a number of issues.

1.   *Is it difficult to measure the value added by the provider?*

If there aren't clear measures to see what value is being added then it makes the service difficult to price and makes SLAs to monitor performance difficult to agree.

2.   *Are service outcomes highly dependent on the performance of other services?*

Services that depend on others are difficult to incentivise and measure objectively. The situation can arise where poor performance by another service makes it impossible for the supplier to meet targets regardless of their performance. It can also be true that over performance elsewhere can help suppliers meet targets when they haven't really done so under their own steam. All this makes contractual SLAs and incentives difficult to formulate and agree.

3.   *Does delivering the service require investment in highly specific assets?*

If it does require these specific assets (human, technological, infrastructure, specialism etc.) then firstly it makes the cost of contracting high. The supplier will require investment to meet the requirements which will be reflected in the price. It also gives the incumbent a significant advantage at retender meaning that the client may not get the best value.

4.   *Is the service characterised by high demand uncertainty?*

This type of service places a high degree of risk on the supplier that will be reflected in the price unless the client mitigates that risk for them.

5.   *Is the service characterised by high policy uncertainty?*

If policy is likely to change impacting on a contractual relationship then there is the potential for high exit costs or change control for the client.

6.   *Is the service inherently governmental?*

Does the service involve key policy decisions, is it central to law and order capability or does it work with a duty to protect the public, if so a contract may not work.

The report suggests offsetting factors that may impact on the cost of transition which are:

- Is there an existing supply of high-quality providers?

- Is there an existing workforce (either in public or private sectors) with adequate skills and capabilities to deliver high-quality services?

- Does the government have the organisational capability to design and monitor the use of contractual mechanisms?

- Does the government have enough information about cost and quality to measure provider performance?

The report does suggest some mitigation to the list of six issues but I would like to add some of my own to those.

1. *Is it difficult to measure the value added by the provider?*

   If the service value is difficult to measure can you use proxy measures? These can sometimes be dangerous as they may encourage the wrong type of behaviour in the supplier but they can also give valuable measurement. However, in some cases it is acceptable to just not measure the value added. You can specify what needs to be done without worrying about quality as long as you have a contract that is flexible as far as termination and is also flexible as far as setting the measurements later. A service such as office cleaning is very difficult to set quality targets for, the best approach is to retain the ability to change suppliers. The threat of losing the contract works better than contract penalties.

2. *Are service outcomes highly dependent on the performance of other services?*

   One of the main mitigations for this is to lump the dependent services into one contract to ensure that the interdependencies don't matter as they are performed by the same organisation.

This does have downsides in that it places all the eggs in one basket and means you may not have best in class for each part of the service (see later chapter on multi-sourcing) but it does mitigate the initial problem.

One of the ways National Rail Enquiries approach this issue is to include requirements to cooperate with others suppliers and to include Operational Level Agreements (OLAs). These OLAs tie suppliers' SLAs into an overall outcome. It is in the interests of all suppliers to cooperate to achieve these as all their contracts include these measures.

3.   *Does delivering the service require investment in highly specific assets?*

The chief risk here is giving too much power to an incumbent supplier so owning the asset takes away that power. The obvious mitigation here is to own the asset. Owning the asset also allows for better continuity as the asset used by the next supplier is the same as the previous supplier. This may hold back innovation but there is nothing to stop the client investing in updating the asset to achieve that innovation.

National Rail Enquiries use this principle as far as possible with IP. If new software is being developed National Rail Enquiries will own the intellectual property rights of that software, allowing them to move it to another supplier if the contract changes. This isn't always possible as one of the advantages of outsourcing is suppliers bringing in pre-existing Intellectual Property, but it can help mitigate much of the risk in this area.

Similarly public-sector organisations very often enter into management contracts where the client provides the assets and the supplier manages them.

4.   *Is the service characterised by high demand uncertainty?*

This is an area of risk management. I have strong views on this and believe that suppliers should only bear the risk on areas they have control of. The National Rail Enquiries call centres are a good example of this where demand is reasonably steady and predictable until there is some disruption. Snow in the South East of England on a weekday can send call volumes through the roof. Because of this National Rail Enquiries protect the supplier by limiting the variance of calls they are expected to deal with inside the contractual SLAs. Over that band and National Rail Enquiries require only "best endeavours".

Also in the call centres long-term volume is uncertain. National Rail Enquiries have invested heavily in self-service channels and the proportion of calls to total contacts has gone from originally being 100 per cent to less than 0.75 per cent in 2013. This is out of the supplier's control, and is driven by the client, so the structure of charges is split into set-up, fixed costs, variable costs and incentives. A fixed set-up charge means that the supplier will not over or under recover the set-up costs by trying to incorporate them into the call charges. Their risk is that the set-up costs will be greater than they bid, which is in their control.

Fixed costs (management, IT, floor space, etc.) are set for six-month periods on the assumption that over that time they can be flexed. For example as call volumes fall and less floor space is required the call centre supplier can reduce floor space over a period of time. They just can't do it on a day-to-day basis.

The variable cost of a call is down to the supplier. That is training and resourcing correctly.

5.   *Is the service characterised by high policy uncertainty?*

The use of the word "policy" makes this sound like it only applies to government but it also applies to the private sector. Companies that may change their minds on strategy will be exposed to additional costs in outsourcing. If you contract out a service for three years and decide you no longer need it six months later there will be a cost.

My advice in this situation is to make sure the contract has early termination payments. There will be a cost but it is easier to negotiate these before you sign the contract than after.

This is probably preferable to short-term contracts which lessen the incentive for the supplier to invest time and effort into making it work.

The report from the Institute of Government (Gash and Panchamia 2013) suggests the sensible mitigation of getting a broad consensus on policy before the service is contracted to lessen the risk of change.

There are examples of government projects failing because of a lack of political consensus behind them. Some think that this has contributed to the issues with the Affordable Health Act in the US (Booty 2013). In any case policy uncertainty and a lack of consensus behind a service increases the risks, whether it is in the public or private sector.

6.   *Is the service inherently governmental?*

This strikes at one of the key issues on the decision to outsource. Are you outsourcing out functions of your business to make you more efficient or are outsourcing your core business. There is nothing to say you can't outsource core functions but there is a higher risk of loss of control of your business if you do.

On the factors affecting the cost of transition the report has some comments to which I have added some of my own.

- Is there an existing supply of high-quality providers?

    - Markets vary but if there is a large number of quality providers in the market then choice will be higher and competition greater. Also the ability to swap in the future is greater.
    - In this instance contracting out services becomes more attractive.

- Is there an existing workforce (either in public or private sectors) with adequate skills and capabilities to deliver high-quality services?

    - If this workforce exists already then outsourcing is more attractive. Areas where the skills are in short supply means that outsourcers may struggle to attract the right staff, and in any case competition may be limited leading to higher prices and less options, both initially and when looking to retender.

- Does the client have the organisational capability to design and monitor the use of contractual mechanisms?

  - A recurring theme is the skill set that the client has to commission and run outsourcing contracts. If this skill set doesn't exist then the client should seek to acquire the skills before embarking on a plan of outsourcing.
  - Again this isn't a reason not to outsource but is a reason to make sure you are ready to outsource.

- Does the client have enough information about cost and quality to measure provider performance?

  - As well as having the skills to commission and manage an outsourcing relationship do you have the data to be able to set meaningful service levels and to monitor those? If you don't then you should consider taking the time to develop that information so that you can maximise the benefit of an outsourcing arrangement.

Summary

This is a reasonably short list of the areas that can make outsourcing arrangements underperform or even fail.

However, whilst it is important to understand these issues it is more important to get the outsourcing strategy and approach to that strategy right. If you get that right, many of these issues fall away and the next few chapters address the issue of outsourcing strategy and the approach to that strategy.

PART III
Models of Outsourcing

Chapter 8
Single-Sourcing and Other Models

Single-sourcing is generally meant to mean sourcing a whole service from a single supplier. A good example, and one I will use in this and the next chapter, would be a website where you have one supplier delivering the customer-facing service. They take care of design, static data, dynamic information, hosting, support, etc.

The following diagram shows the contractual relationships in a single-sourced arrangement. There are a number of different services being supplied by the subcontractors but the client only has a relationship with the prime contractor.

The example here is how National Rail Enquires used to deliver the website www.nationalrail.co.uk.

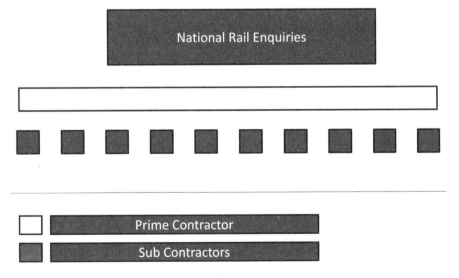

Figure 8.1   Single-Sourcing Model

In this example National Rail Enquiries had no direct relationship with the layer of subcontractors. Everything went through the prime contractor and that prime contractor was responsible for delivery of the whole service.

It is important to understand that single-sourcing isn't handing over your whole business to one supplier but it is handing over a whole service. However that service could be key to your business so the ability to shift responsibility onto a prime contractor is, ultimately, limited.

Single-sourcing is seen as a more risk-averse approach to outsourcing, although I would disagree as the ability to transfer the risk is questionable, and is quite prevalent in the public sector, although this is changing. It is also popular where the service being outsourced isn't seen as being key or core to the business. It takes a non-essential service and shifts it off to an outsourcer to run. The client involvement can become minimal if that is what the client wants.

Areas where an essential service would be outsourced on a single-sourced basis would be the example of cleaning services. It would be unusual to outsource the office cleaning but not leave it all to one supplier, although that does happen. Sometimes companies will have multiple suppliers for a relatively straightforward and non-core service such as cleaning if it is a very large contract or is geographically spread. In the first instance the client may feel the contract is too large for one organisation or they wish to retain some competitive tension between suppliers. In the second it may be that a single supplier doesn't have the geographical spread or it is just better to use local suppliers. However, it is usual for services such as this to be on a single source arrangement.

An example of single-sourcing in a more key service would be the way in which National Rail Enquiries used to run their website. They had a single outsourcer to provide the whole thing. Hosting, website, journey planner, static data (things like information on stations such as parking and booking office opening times), design etc. were all contracted through the same company. The single-sourcing company didn't provide everything itself, as it subcontracted some parts of the service to other suppliers, but it held the contract with the client for the overall service.

The single-sourcing model did have advantages for National Rail Enquiries. There was one port of call for any problems. There was no issue about finding who was to blame and take the issue to them. With only one contractor it wasn't our problem to find out where the problem was, we just had to raise it.

Contract management was also easy. With only one prime supplier the management overhead was low. We were also dealing with a substantial organisation so the risk of financial problems in the supplier was less and continuity of service more certain.

However this approach did have problems.

Firstly the rate of change was slow. Take for example a change to the layout of the website. We would take this to the supplier as a change request but they were unable to implement this on their own. They needed to involve the design company and perhaps the hosting organisation and maybe others. If we didn't like the result then the whole process would have to be restarted. Because of this the change process became long and cumbersome, and we were losing competitive edge because we couldn't get the changes in quickly enough for our customers.

It was also expensive. When the cost came in from the design company the prime contractor passed this on with a margin so we were paying margin on margin. This made us less inclined to make changes, compounding the slow change process detailed above.

The single-sourcing model really didn't work for us and we decided to change to multi-sourcing which, we feel, has the advantages as explained in the next chapter.

Whilst we chose multi-sourcing there are others we could have used had they been suitable. Paul Corrall describes a number of different options (Corrall 2013).

Corrall writes that the reduction in size of contract values has led to requirements for more adaptable sourcing models. He cites single-sourcing and multi-sourcing but also:

- Gain share. This is where the supplier's revenue is linked to the gain that the client realises (Lawrence 2011). In many cases this gain is a cost saving but not always. The benefit can be measured in other ways including improvement in the quality of the service or customer satisfactions levels. This has advantages where:

  - The supplier is heavily focused on achieving the gain for the client.

- The contract is de-risked from a client point of view in that they aren't going to pay fees if the benefits aren't realised.
- Actual gains are tracked, making it much easier to justify the decision (or see if it didn't deliver).
- You don't need a large budget to start the engagement.

- However Lawrence also sees problems with the model.

  - He sees the model as encouraging "casino consulting" because of the risk placed on the supplier. No gain no fee.
  - If the supplier finds an easy saving route the client can end up paying a disproportionate amount of money that it could have saved under a different model.
  - If it is purely based on cost savings then issues such as quality, customer satisfaction, future development, strategy etc. are all ignored.
  - It encourages a model for the supplier where cost savings are related to effort. The supplier will want to take the "low hanging fruit" and book the easy savings with little incentive to go for the longer term, harder or smaller savings.
  - Failure is invisible, success visible. The client does not know where the gains are. If they did they wouldn't be paying the premium of gain share to get those gains. Without that visibility the savings are clear as the supplier will make sure they are seen. However failure, such as overlooking savings, will not be clear.
  - Gain share can cause budget problems as the savings and benefits may not coincide with the fees being charged from a timing perspective. When this is across functions the budgeting can be especially confused.
  - There is a requirement to calculate the gains, which takes effort that, in itself, brings no benefit to the business. There are also many instances where this isn't a straightforward calculation and dispute resolution can absorb more unproductive time for both sides.
  - It doesn't engender a collaborative approach. The issue over who is to gain credit for a saving isn't just status but, in this model, becomes a financial issue. Suppliers want to be paid as much as possible and clients can be unwilling to agree fees based on savings that they believe were not entirely of the supplier's making.

- Gain share puts pressure on long-term goals as it tends to encourage short saving over the long-term good of the business. Indeed this is another area that can lead to dispute where the client is unwilling to realise short savings that it believes will have a detrimental effect in the long term.
- In other areas such as sales and marketing the "commission only" model has become unfashionable. Driving people purely on results can lead to less than acceptable performance. Gain share is the outsourcing equivalent of the old "commission only" remuneration package.

This list of issues may seem to be damning of the model but it really serves as a memorandum to help decide what you outsource under this model. Knowing the problems is key to deciding if it will work for you in a particular service.

In some areas the gain share model does work. It can encourage significant business change that the client may not be able to drive internally (Overby 2012). Stephanie Overby's article on CIO.com covers many of the problems highlighted by Lawrence but also states that the model can encourage cooperation as the goals of both sides are aligned. However it also adds another issue described as the "second-year blues". If the first year is really successful the client is going to want to make the year two targets harder. If it isn't successful the supplier will want to make them easier. It can be a bit like negotiating a complete new contract after one year.

There are other outsourcing models to be considered.

- One model is creating a mutual. This is where an organisation allows the staff to take over a service whether on their own or in a partnership with a third party such as an outsourcing provider. This has many advantages as the staff are motivated by running the service for their own benefit. The motivation benefits the client and there is a social value to letting the in-house team take over the service. However one of the downsides is that you do not get the bought in expertise of an outsourcing service provider which is why this usually works better for the client as a hybrid solution with third parties involved as well.

- Joint ventures are another solution to outsourcing. This is where the client and supplier form a joint venture company to provide the service. I worked in a joint venture in Schlumberger where the communications of Schlumberger were handled by a joint venture company owned by Schlumberger and Cable and Wireless. Schlumberger gained the communications expertise of Cable and Wireless and Cable and Wireless gained access and experience in geographical markets where traditionally they weren't strong or, in some cases, not there at all.

Ultimately the joint venture between Schlumberger and Cable and Wireless was dissolved as the aims of the two organisations were diverging. Because of the value of the data that Schlumberger were dealing with they were becoming more interested in the security of the communications whereas Cable and Wireless were looking to expand their global footprint. This is a common issue where joint ventures are formed to deliver specific services. The underlying strategy of the partners can cause the joint venture to dissolve as the different strategies want to take the collaboration in different directions.

- Social impact bonds, also known as "pay for success" bonds or "social benefit" bonds are another growing solution. These are defined as "a contract with the public sector in which a commitment is made to pay for improved social outcomes that result in public sector savings" (Social Impact Bond n.d.).

These are based on the principle that investing in the prevention of social and health problems ultimately saves the government money. Often governments don't have the funds or innovative flair for this initial investment to work. So the governments commit to use a proportion of the savings that come from this prevention to reward the investors who have funded the early work.

For example a programme set up for prisoner rehabilitation may reduce prisoner numbers and allow the government to shut down prisons with a resulting saving to the public purse.

This type of agreement allows government to partner with innovative service providers and other investors whilst ensuring that the taxpayer does not pay unless there is a demonstrable success.

These are relatively new with the first announcement of such a bond in March 2010 by the UK Justice Secretary for a prisoner rehabilitation programme, and in the US in 2012 with the Second Chance Act. In August 2012 Massachusetts issued a competitive procurement to obtain services using social innovation financing followed on by New York with a $9.6 million social bond for prisoner rehabilitation.

This type of agreement removes much of the risk from the public sector as they only pay for effective services. The provider is motivated to produce these effective services so that they can recover their investment and make a return.

The downside of these arrangements includes the fact that they only work if the success can be measured. Areas where the success and outcomes cannot be measured will not benefit from this model.

There is also a concern that it leads to a reduction in public accountability. Government is devolving responsibility to other businesses for what is essentially part of maintaining a civil society.

- As has been happening for a number of years another outsourcing model is offshoring. This is not just for labour arbitrage (moving to countries where the labour is cheaper) but is also to help the client deliver multi-lingual services. It can also be used to concentrate on national skill sets. Some cultures are better at certain aspects of business (IT, customer service, design etc.) and offshoring services allows you to set up functions in countries that may fit the skill set better than the home country. It is also a fact that for multinationals "home country" is a hazy term.

Offshoring is much maligned in the press for the Indian call centre stories (although the Indian call centres for National Rail Enquiries score higher customer satisfaction scores than the UK centres ever did). But there is more to it than that. Offshoring now includes business processes, finance and admin and legal outsourcing. Many companies offshore design services and, as you would expect, manufacturing.

This increase in offshoring can create centres of excellence helping to deliver better quality as well as cost reduction.

- Service integration. I will cover this in specific detail when I look at the future and explain recent developments in National Rail Enquiries, however technological advances and the move to more multi-sourced models brings in the possibility of a service integration layer. The client has to make a decision as to how much of this is delivered by them and how much by outsourcers. I will explain the National Rail Enquiries approach to that question later but, even then, that is only my view at this time. Technologies can change for the client, supplier and end user and the systems to deliver a service or product to the end user can also change, so the whole issue of service integration is one that will continue to develop.

- Shared service centres help harmonise services and deliver best practice. It delivers a central resource when needed that may not be practical to maintain at a smaller level of operation. Also taking these services into a central operation frees up the delivery staff to do what they do best.

  Shared service centres do not necessarily lead to reduced staff (although this does happen). However, they do take the admin out of the local operations and allow them the freedom to concentrate on the core business.

- Robotic automation and the implementation of a virtual workforce can lead to significant cost savings and can be delivered in a very short timescale.

  "Robot" is mainly used as a metaphor and reflects the use of technology to mimic or replace a function that would normally be performed by a person (Robotic Automation Software n.d.).

  The technology to do this generally requires an outsourcer to provide the service as there is a significant investment in developing such systems and so it is likely to be uneconomic for individual clients to go it on their own.

  This technology generally improves consistency, speed and cuts costs. Outsourcing in this area can be roughly split in to front of house and back office.

Front-of-house examples are things like IVR voice recognition, and the rate that people are becoming more technically savvy is helping this area. People are far more agreeable to self-service customer service than they would have been a few years ago. National Rail Enquiries used to be 100 per cent person-to-person call centres but in 2013 more than 99.25 per cent of customer contacts to come through the self-service channels.

The back-office examples would include Optical Character Recognition (OCR) in order to input data into systems. The characters on documents, for example supplier invoices, are recognised automatically and input into the system to avoid manual input.

- Lastly don't forget insourcing and having the in-house option. The other models here are using third parties but you should usually at least consider the in-house option. It is a model that sometimes works well and even at National Rail Enquiries we made a decision to bring the display ad sales back in-house. In-house can sometimes be the best option but in some circumstances it can be the only option as an outsourced solution may not exist.

Summary

There are many outsourcing models that suppliers and clients can use and they all have advantages and disadvantages. Single-sourcing remains popular in many organisations and in many situations. Indeed in some areas National Rail Enquiries (the organisation I hold up as having a multi-sourcing strategy that has helped it achieve success) has dropped the number of suppliers. Specifically in the call centres the reduction in call volumes has led to a reduction in suppliers down to one, although they do still multi-source as they have some of the services around the call centre operations (including communications and journey planning software) contracted with other suppliers. As can be seen you should be prepared to look at different sourcing strategies should the need arise.

However it is widely recognised that one of the most popular trends in outsourcing is the move to multi-sourcing, which has been a key factor in the success of National Rail Enquiries. It is this model that I will discuss in the next chapter.

Chapter 9

Multi-Sourcing and the National Rail Enquiries Experience

Multi-sourcing is where the client has the relationship with the individual subcontractors as per the model in Figure 9.1. The prime contractor is taken out of the equation (although it may still be supplying services as one of the contractors) and the client has the direct relationship. It is a more selective approach (selective sourcing is often used in describing multi-sourcing as well as the sometimes used phrase of tower sourcing) where the client is picking suppliers for discrete parts of the service rather than for the whole thing.

Again I use the example of the National Rail Enquires website, where we now have a direct relationship with what used to be the subcontractors to the prime contractor. The client now takes on the role of systems or service integrator. The same functions are there, as with the single-sourcing model, but we contract directly for those functions.

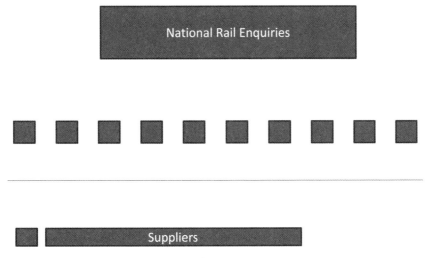

Figure 9.1   Multi-Sourcing Model

When compared to the single-sourcing figure in the previous chapter we are just taking out the prime contractor and contracting with the actual suppliers of the services directly. The various services supplied under the direct contracts in Figure 9.1 include:

- Hosting;

- Help desk support and triage;

- Journey planning;

- Maintaining static data;

- Design;

- Ad serving;

- Provision of user interface;

- Sales hand-offs to Train Operating Companies;

- Affiliate arrangements such as hotel and search revenue streams;

- Help facilities including an avatar;

- Station journey planning for people with reduced mobility.

This model has a number of advantages but also disadvantages. The advantages include:

- You are dealing with the experts. In the example of a website the people who do the design contract directly with the client rather than through a prime contractor. That direct contact allows them to better understand the client's needs and goals and so helps them to better meet those goals. From the client side they have the feedback of experts. This may raise issues or opportunities that the client wouldn't have thought of otherwise.

  In the case of the National Rail Enquiries website they deal directly with the design agency who are experts in designing websites. The feedback they get from them and the understanding of their business that they give to them is essential in the success of the relationship.

• Picking individual suppliers allows you to pick the best in class without being restricted to suppliers picked by a prime contractor. You have the freedom to shop around and pick the best supplier for each individual part of the service and pick suppliers that you feel can grow with you. A prime contractor may pick suppliers based on existing relationships as this keeps their management overhead down and improves their purchasing power.

• Change control in a multi-sourcing arrangement is quicker. Using the example of website design again National Rail Enquiries discuss what they want to do with the website directly with the relevant suppliers. Ideas are thrashed out with the design agency, and the journey planning supplier and user interface supplier are involved to help National Rail Enquiries understand the practical and technical impacts of what they are discussing.

It isn't a case of going through a prime contractor, with the misunderstandings that can arise and that only serve to lengthen the change process, but is more a case of direct engagement and feedback to get the change agreed as soon as possible.

• Moving suppliers is quicker and easier. Rather than have an entire service with one supplier, as you do with single-sourcing arrangements, with multi-sourcing you have the service cut into smaller parts and with different suppliers. The consequence of this is that if something isn't working, and doesn't seem likely to work, you don't have to retender the whole service but just a small part of it. This makes the change quicker and something that can be done with much less risk on the service. It also reduces the risk to the client of a supplier failing as you can shift the service quickly.

• The fact that the service is split up into smaller chunks of work opens the door for smaller suppliers. Businesses that don't have the staff, financial clout or breadth of experience to deliver the whole service can get direct contracts with the client under a multi-sourcing model. This can help innovation but is certainly good for the market place as it helps develop new suppliers and increase competition. This is an area where even small clients can help the market stewardship that is so important to government outsourcing.

- Following on from the previous point, multi-sourcing lets you fine tune the service better. If something isn't working, say the hosting, then you can retender that part of the service to improve it. You don't have to retender the whole thing which may mean you retendering things that were working fine.

- The margin on margin is avoided. Going back to the design example the design company obviously add a mark up to their costs but when going through a prime contractor they also need to add a mark-up. This escalates the cost whilst adding little value.

There are of course disadvantages to multi-sourcing:

- The risk of failure falls more squarely on the client. With a prime contractor you have a single point of blame. If something doesn't work in the service there is one company to yell at and one company whose responsibility it is to fix it. In a multi-sourcing environment the onus is on the client to find out where it went wrong and work with the individual supplier or suppliers to get it fixed.

  I have never really seen this as much of a disadvantage as the reasons behind a fault and who is to blame are largely irrelevant. The client is responsible for the service to its customers so if there is a failure it is the client organisation who will be held accountable regardless of what outsourcing arrangements there are behind the scenes. The end customer doesn't really care who is at fault when something goes wrong and the onus is still on the client to fix things regardless of the sourcing model.

- Multi-sourcing can produce friction between suppliers as many of them will be direct competitors put into a situation where they need to cooperate. They also may be some friction on where the credit for success gets recognized. With a number of suppliers working on a service it is sometimes difficult to allocate fault but it can also be difficult to allocate credit.

  Whilst this is an issue it can be dealt with through proper governance processes. It doesn't have to be a major issue.

- However, there is one major criticism of multi-sourcing that I fully agree with. That is the management overhead it places on the client. Dealing with multiple suppliers requires not only more management resource but a different skill set from single-sourcing, as you need to be much more hands on.

This issue of management overhead brings us to the approach to governance by the client. This is one of the key success factors for outsourcing and this is particularly true in multi-sourcing.

The UK National Outsourcing Association lists ten objectives from the governance of outsourcing contracts (National Outsourcing Association 2013a):

- Focus on the strategic business objectives and imperatives;

- Nurture and enhance the relationship between provider and customer;

- Enable the delivery of quality services to meet business needs;

- Satisfy the expectations of the stakeholders;

- Enable effective decision making and mitigate risk;

- Foster the creation of value and enable innovative practices to flourish;

- Enable effective communication;

- Establish trust and confidence between all parties;

- Provide oversight and direction;

- Maintain stewardship, responsibility and accountability.

The building of an effective governance relationship starts before the contract is signed, indeed before it is even awarded. The client needs to drive this by being open with the suppliers about their approach to governance and to explain how they will approach it during the contract. They need to control expectations and make sure the suppliers know what will be expected of them. Don't be unrealistic but at the same time make sure that they are clear on the level of value they expect. It is important to get this balance right.

There needs to be an understanding of what the business relationship will be. Who will be dealing with who and at what level. If possible the people who will be running the service from both sides need to be involved. This is a good time to tick the "like, trust, believe" box in the clients tender evaluation. Business requirements change over time so you need to know that the supplier will not just meet the requirements in the tender document but will also work with you to meet the changes into the future. If you think the supplier is just there to meet the tender requirements and try to expand their business by moving on to pick up other business elsewhere you need to think if they are the guys for you. If you believe that they want to meet the tender requirements but work with you to expand your business and build their business through your success then you may have found a long-term partner.

The suppliers also need to know what is expected from them in the governance commitment. At National Rail Enquiries we explained our governance mechanisms that require supplier input. One of these is the six-monthly supplier days. This is usually two days with an overnight dinner for socialising and getting to know each other. The days consist of presentations from the National Rail Enquiries team on future plans and what our key performance indicators (KPIs) are and how we are doing against them. You can't expect a supplier to help you take your business forward if they don't know what your KPIs and targets are, what issues you face and what your development roadmap and future plans are. Sometimes innovation comes as a bolt of lightning or the metaphorical light bulb above the head but most times it is an idea to take forward an existing idea. Letting the suppliers know what you are planning allows them to think of innovations and improvements along the lines of your future plans. Also you can't expect suppliers to help you meet your KPIs if you don't tell them what they are. National Rail Enquiries tell them what they are, how they are doing against them and give details about how they have got to where they are and the difficulties they see in improving on them.

National Rail Enquiries multi-source so you have a room full of suppliers, none of whom supply a complete service. That is why part of the supplier days is having break-out sessions where different groups of suppliers get together to brainstorm problems such as the achievement of KPIs and the development of the roadmap and future plans. These break-out sessions have been very successful in not only creating ideas for National Rail Enquiries but also in bringing the suppliers together to work as teams. There is obviously some competitive tension between the suppliers but overall National Rail Enquiries have found this a very successful governance mechanism.

Once the contract is awarded the governance moves into a phase of closer engagement, where staff from the client work with the supplier to help ensure the delivery time scales and service quality targets are met. This approach also helps to highlight problems early on. A Finance Director I once worked with told me "I can cope with problems. What I can't handle are surprises". Keeping close to the supplier during the implementation can help delivery but at the end of the day that is the supplier's responsibility. What it really helps with is avoiding the surprises.

Moving on from the running of the contract the client needs to plan the exit management. Whilst we all want long-term, successful outsourcing contracts they do come to an end and that needs to be planned for. Establishing the exit plan from the start of the contract is good governance. The client knows what the supplier will do on exit and the supplier knows what is expected of it. Both sides can cost this in and the exit is a known exercise with, hopefully, no surprises. When you are moving from one supplier to another the last thing you need is problems and disputes with the outgoing supplier.

However writing about the importance of good governance in outsourcing, and especially multi-sourcing models, is all well and good. But how do you achieve it?

The simple answer to the question is people and systems. Glenn Hickling discusses the skill sets needed (Hickling 2013). He points out research from the International Association of Outsourcing Professionals, which found that 63 per cent of companies believed they lose an average of 25 per cent of contract value from poor governance. Good governance is to a large extent about skill set, and Hickling describes seven governors.

1.   The one with the iron fist:

       This is a requirement to be strong with the supplier. Make sure you get what you are paying for and what was agreed. He points out the way suppliers have very bright people to sell the service but these people move on once the sale is made. Insist on continuity, set out what the contact points will be and make sure you have people that you want as your contacts throughout the agreement.

2.   The one with internal discipline:

The client needs to do what needs to be done as well. It won't just happen, and if the client does sit back then failures can slip into a blame game which just burns time and effort. You need to get your own house in order, make sure your own people know what they need to do and put someone in charge who can make sure it does get done.

3.   The one with the velvet glove:

This is about soft skills such as conflict resolution, problem solving and strategic thinking. Listen to the supplier as well as your own staff and be a problem solver. Strength is important but use emotional intelligence, tact and diplomacy to get a resolution. As Hickling puts it "Blessed are the peacemakers. Nowhere more so than in a complex web of multi-sourcing".

4.   The wise one with the wisdom of the past:

Learn from the past. Outsourcing has been around a long time and there are plenty of examples of good practice and bad practice. Chapters 6 and 7 have plenty of pointers on what to look out for and why things go wrong. You don't have to start from scratch and if you don't want to learn there are plenty of people out there with lengthy experience of outsourcing. If in doubt get them in.

5.   The one who can see the future:

Keep up to date as much as you can and be prepared for change. This is partly having the contract terms to allow this change to happen but also having the governance skills to see change, evaluate the benefit and work to incorporate it if the change is beneficial. Share your future plans with the supplier so that they can help you achieve those plans. They can't help you if they don't know and not all innovation can come from the supplier.

6.   The outsourcing prophet:

Spread the good word internally and communicate goals and values to everyone. Multi-sourcing arrangements are complex and communications need to reflect this complexity. Make sure that the communications are open and honest without falling into a blame game. This will earn credibility and help the smooth running of the relationship.

7.   Doctrine and documents:

"A single version of the truth" (Vagadia 2013) is the holy grail. Having all the information available and the system followed will help make outsourcing work but very often isn't followed. In a Gartner survey 53 per cent of organisations don't believe that "they have any experienced outsourcing governance". Systems and documentation will give them much of that experience as it will be spread around the business and available to all. The doctrine can be spread through systems rather than through an individual's knowhow. This will not only help with the service to hand but also with future work.

My own personal experience has convinced me on the importance of governance in outsourcing and the importance in having the right skills. The more you outsource and the more complex the outsourcing arrangements become then the more governance skills are required.

Chris Halward writes about the science of relationship management (Halward 2012). The ability to manage relationships across multiple teams from different suppliers needs a science behind it and a bit of art. Chris lists areas such as development processes for competency and trust, analysis of business value, managing stakeholders, driving improvement and innovation, review and benchmarking and monitoring the relationship. This is the science of managing the relationships but don't forget the art. The ability to get along, persuade, convince, see the other side, develop relationships and to implement conflict resolution – these are as important, if not more, than the science.

National Rail Enquiries have changed the nature of their staffing to reflect the need for greater governance, and a different skill set, to cope with multi-sourcing. In the past five years the balance of staff between those with rail expertise and those with outsourcing expertise has moved from over 40 per cent having rail experience, to less than 25 per cent. The increase in those with outsourcing skills has been in contract and service management, project management, process management and service delivery with some increase in procurement and business development. But above all has been the need to introduce the soft skills of conflict resolution and persuasion. Relationship development is an important skill and working with a large number of suppliers makes it difficult to implement. In order to effectively manage a multi-sourcing business you need to have all these skills, on top of the processes, to be able to effectively manage the relationships and to be able to move the business forward with the suppliers you have.

This change in the National Rail Enquiries skills set is shown in Figure 9.2.

A similar change should be seen in other organisations that are moving to multi-sourcing so that the governance can be effective.

BP is a particular example of successful multi-sourcing having taken hundreds of millions of pounds off its costs through successful outsourcing (Flinders 2013). However you don't have to be a huge corporation like BP with massive resources to have successful multi-sourcing. National Rail Enquiries employ less than 30 people and they can manage a multi-sourcing environment, albeit nowhere on the scale of BP.

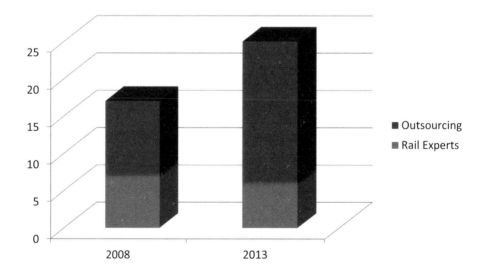

Figure 9.2   National Rail Enquiries Staff Skill Set

Summary

The move to multi-sourcing at National Rail Enquiries has involved a transformation of the business. Not only is it a change in process it is a change in structure, approach and attitudes. This change has not been easy but the benefits are clear with a huge reduction in costs on the back of an expanding business. They now have a much faster change control process, better systems and far more flexibility than they had before and this has been seen in the success of the business.

In the right circumstances multi-sourcing can deliver huge benefits but you need to have the right approach, make the changes to your own organization and operate under a solid framework with a sound governance structure to fully realise those benefits.

Chapter 10
A Suggested Sourcing Framework

The Department of Work and Pensions in the UK is leading the government push to outsourcing with 39 per cent of their running costs outsourced. The department is a huge operation with over 860 job centres around the country, working with over 100,000 people and amounts totalling billions of pounds each year. Their approach to outsourcing is influenced by government policy and EU law but is still highly flexible. However, the work at the Institute for Government shows that what is also needed is a framework for best practice. There is the need for a best practice framework whatever model or degree of outsourcing you choose but this is especially important where the outsourcing is wider and/or uses one of the more complex models such as multi-sourcing.

The National Outsourcing Association (NOA) in the UK runs professional development programmes for outsourcing professionals through the NOA Pathway. One of the key cornerstones of this training is the Outsourcing Life Cycle.

The Life Cycle looks at outsourcing as a continuum rather than start, running of the service and exit. It is one continuous process rather than discrete, isolated projects. The NOA believe that at the core of this ongoing process is strategic leadership, linking everything together and moving them forward. It focuses on relationships and change management. It is not meant to be an outsourcing methodology but rather a framework around which methodologies can be developed.

The Life Cycle has three key principles.

Firstly there are the relationships. The National Outsourcing Association has research that shows that excellent relationships are essential for success in outsourcing. Arm's length management is not effective, especially where the services being outsourced are more strategic. There is a need to strive for good relationships between both teams, and between individuals, to aid success.

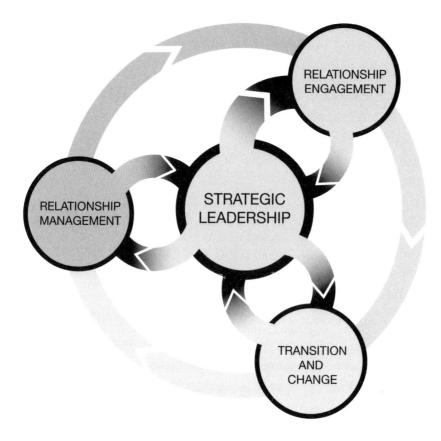

**Figure 10.1   NOA Outsourcing Life Cycle (National Outsourcing
Association 2012)**

Next is the principle of alignment. Your sourcing strategy needs to be aligned with your corporate strategy. The corporate strategy may involve reducing costs, increasing revenue, increasing global reach, diversification, increasing and/or improving use of technology, improving competitive differentiators, etc. Whatever your strategy both sides need to understand those strategic goals, align needs and capabilities and ensure that these are clearly enshrined in the contracts.

Finally there is a word that is used often in this book and that is governance. It is good governance that ensures that the relationships flourish and that the alignment of the outsourcing and corporate strategy starts right and stays right.

The Life Cycle is about the strategy, direction and content of an outsourcing arrangement and is a framework around four key stages, shown in Figure 10.1.

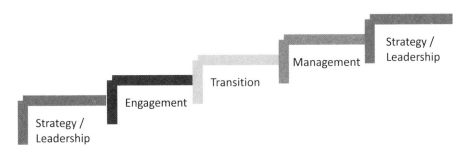

Figure 10.2   Linear Life Cycle (National Outsourcing Association 2012)

The NOA Life Cycle maps the outsourcing process from cradle to grave. It takes the process from the initial strategic discussions to the exit from the relationship. It is written from the viewpoint of the client, but can be used from the supplier perspective.

Figure 10.2 describes the Life Cycle as a linear process.

This is not a unique way of looking at outsourcing or indeed many business change management processes. Start with a strategic review, move on to engaging the resources, transition to the new vision, manage the ongoing process and review strategy. However the NOA Life Cycle framework places strategy and leadership at the centre of the cycle. This is to highlight the need for strategy and leadership to be an ongoing review at the heart of the process and not just something that is done at certain stages. It runs through the core of the whole life cycle of an outsourcing strategy. Practitioners such as myself have seen situations where this is not the case and where the process can lose focus on what the overall company objectives are. You can often end up delivering something very useful but not aligned with where you started and not aligned with the company-wide objectives. When you are building a house you don't look at the plans, go away and build the house and then come back and check the plans to see if what you built was what was in the plans. You check back at every point in the process. That is how it is with an outsourcing strategy.

The Life Cycle also emphasises the importance of relationships. It starts with the relationship engagement where the future relationships are established. This is led by the client and part of it is the selection of the supplier. National Rail Enquiries have one of their selection criteria as "like, trust, believe". Basically, can we get on with these guys, do we think they are in it for the long run and view this as an adaptable relationship, or are they in it to deliver a service to a set of service levels? However, although led by the client, the relationship engagement is also important for the supplier. An agreement isn't signed by one party and the supplier needs to be on board as well. The procurement process at National Rail Enquiries is a very reiterative one so that both sides not only get comfortable with the details of what is being delivered but also comfortable with who they are going to be working with and what the expectations are.

The next wheel around strategic leadership is transition and change. Transition and change are obviously going to happen, as you are moving the service at the beginning and it is highly unlikely that the service will stay the same throughout. Most outsourcing suppliers will be good at transition and change but it is important to realise that this isn't always the same and the supplier processes have to be adaptable to the clients' specific needs. Some transitions are easy and some are not, and it is up to both sides to work together to make sure they both understand where their transition lies and how to make sure that the process is as smooth and effective as possible. There needs to be a similar approach to changes during the agreement. Not all clients are the same and the supplier needs to understand how the client approaches change and the client needs to understand how the supplier approaches change to make sure they are aligned. If they aren't then you need to know how you can get them aligned.

Relationships come up again in the Life Cycle again under relationship management. This is the ongoing process and emphasises the need for ongoing management, including effective communication and facilitation skills, the management of issues and dispute resolution and the ability to view things from the other side to help resolve issues at least when they arise but hopefully before they arise. The relationship management also requires hard skills in commercial and technical areas, it requires good service, project and process management and it also requires good management of the client's own staff.

As shown in the Life Cycle diagram the key stages are:

- Strategic Leadership;

- Relationship Engagement;

- Transition and Change;

- Relationship Management.

Strategic Leadership Phase

This is at the centre of the Life Cycle framework. As highlighted earlier in this book outsourcing should be a strategic decision, a sourcing strategy should be developed in the context of an organisation's strategic goals. The method of outsourcing (or indeed whether or not to outsource) is considered and the current situation reviewed. This review also looks at the risks and opportunities and the value that may be derived from the various strategies. Once a strategy is chosen, the plans and governance are established to deliver this strategy, including the resourcing requirements and strategic leadership required.

POTENTIAL PROBLEMS

- Incomplete, inaccurate, current state analysis;

- Limited vision for desired state;

- Lack of experienced input leading to limited options being considered;

- Oversimplified procurement strategy;

- Lack of challenge to strategy;

- Inadequate business case.

KEY COMPETENCY AREAS

- Organisational analysis;

- Financial modelling;

- Strategy development;

- Business case development;

- PR communication skills;

- Risk man agement;

- Strategic decision making;

- Sourcing option market research;

- Global economics;

- Leadership.

The flow diagram in Figure 10.3 maps out the processes in the strategic leadership phase.

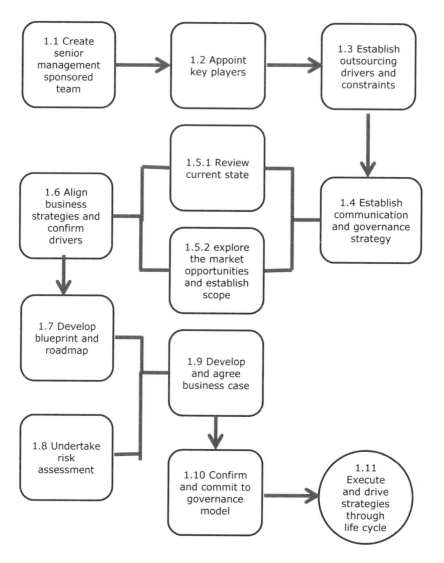

Figure 10.3   The Strategic Leadership Phase

Taking these in turn:

1.1   CREATE SENIOR MANAGEMENT SPONSORED TEAM

The team establishing the outsourcing strategy needs high-level support to ensure that whatever is adopted is well thought through, appropriate for the company-wide strategy and supported at a senior level. This team develops the strategy, gains support for it and then runs the strategy in the long term. The level of senior sponsorship will depend on the impact on the business. In a business such as National Rail Enquiries where nearly everything is outsourced, this team isn't sponsored by senior management, it *is* the senior management.

1.2   APPOINT KEY PLAYERS

The people you appoint need to come from a wide range of disciplines. Often this includes commercial, legal, operational, systems/IT, project management, service delivery, etc. It is OK for people to flit in and out of this team (for example the involvement of a legal counsel may only be needed up front in the tender process and then only when required) but there needs to be a core team whose members stay with the process throughout.

1.3   ESTABLISH OUTSOURCING DRIVERS AND CONSTRAINTS.

The drivers and constraints are key inputs to designing the outsourcing strategy. These drivers and constraints will include:

- What strategies are available (including multi-sourcing, in-house, shared services and many of those listed in Chapter 8);

- The high-level goals of the organisation and the business strategy;

- Lower-level tactical goals;

- The measures of success in the short term, medium term and long term. The actual length of time of these descriptions will vary from business to business but it is important, whatever your timescales are, to look out to different time horizons in deciding a strategy;

- What are the corporate values? Some of these may include a company policy to only use locally sourced services, which places constraints on the outsourcing strategy. They may even include legal restrictions such as data protection which may also constrain the strategy;

- An assessment of the market. Are there a large number of suitable suppliers out there or is it dominated by a few? What are the relative sizes of the organisations and is there a mix of large organisations and SMEs?

- What are the risks and what is the organisation's risk profile? These are relative terms, as what one organisation may see as an insurmountable risk, another will see as manageable;

- What is the exit strategy framework?

I.4   ESTABLISH COMMUNICATION AND GOVERNANCE STRATEGY

Communication is essential to governance and governance is essential to outsourcing success. Communication and governance sit together and you can't have one without the other. However there is a need from the outset to take leadership of this part of the cycle and map out the communication and governance strategy so that it is clear and understood by all. It is not just for those involved in delivering the outsourcing service, both client and supplier side, but for everyone who may be impacted by the outsourcing decision. Outsourcing can conjure up some pretty frightening images for staff in the client's business so it is important to make sure everyone knows what is happening and it isn't left to rumour. On top of this there is often a legal obligation to consult with staff (for example under UK TUPE regulations) so this isn't just good practice.

Because it is so important that communication is clear and consistent it is often best to have one person responsible for this part of the leadership phase.

The governance process needs to be set but does also need to be communicated. It is not much good if nobody knows who is supposed to be doing what.

I.5.I   REVIEW CURRENT STATE

At this point the leadership team is in place, the drivers and constraints of the outsourcing operation have been established and the communications and governance process has been set up. This is a good time to have an initial review of the current state. It helps to clarify the opportunities and challenges that may arise.

One of the areas to cover in the review is thorough engagement with the current team. This can highlight opportunities for development. It can also provide benchmarks so that future success can be better measured. It is important that this stage is undertaken before the organisation is committed to any change such as taking work from in-house to an external supplier, renewing an existing arrangement or changing outsourcing suppliers.

1.5.2   EXPLORE THE MARKET OPPORTUNITIES AND ESTABLISH SCOPE

It is important that before making decisions about outsourcing, changing suppliers or renewing existing suppliers that the client has knowledge of the market. Things change and sometimes they change rapidly so you shouldn't just assume you know what the market is. Very often this will involve advisors who may have knowledge of new technologies (National Rail Enquiries used an external resource when we were looking at changing our hosting arrangements to commodity cloud hosting). They may also operate in the market and know the players helping them to advise the client on the state of the market.

It may also be useful to involve potential suppliers at this stage. It helps them to be involved as early as possible and they may have useful input into the process. A word of warning here, in that suppliers may try to influence the scope and content of the tender to give them an advantage so you need to ensure that you aren't influenced in this way.

However, the input from the suppliers is useful in that it may give you a better understanding of what they can and can't do and what is a reasonable expectation from the service. The last thing you want is to issue a tender and have no viable response because the requirements you have set are unreasonable or uneconomic and the tender has not passed the "bid/no bid" gateway in any of the likely suppliers.

The discussions with suppliers also back up the link between the business strategy and the outsourcing strategy. The NOA has a market cost/capability matrix which is shown in Figure 10.4. This is a very rough matrix of the decision-making process that is helped by an understanding of the market.

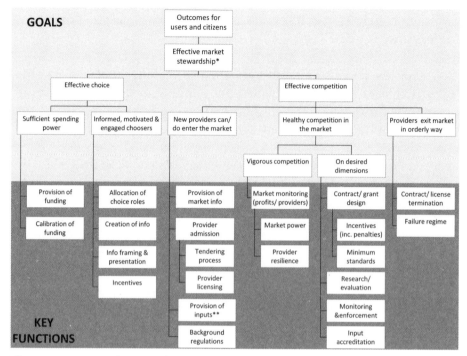

Figure 10.4   Market Cost/Capability Matrix

When compared to internal service delivery an assessment of the market costs and capabilities can help either reaffirm the outsourcing strategy or cause you to rethink that strategy. When the market cost is low and capability high then it would appear to reaffirm the outsourcing decision. However at different ends of the two scales it there may be a case for selective outsourcing or indeed going for the in-house option.

1.6   ALIGN BUSINESS STRATEGIES AND CONFIRM DRIVERS

You should now be in a position to confirm the alignment of the business strategy with the outsourcing strategy and to be able to go back and revalidate the original drivers and constraints. It is good to have these regular checks. As with the building a house analogy you don't want to move too far away from the plan, so regular checks will help keep you on track with the plan.

This is also a good time to revisit the exit strategy. Having explored the market, is the original framework still valid?

I.7   DEVELOP BLUEPRINT AND ROADMAP

This is a document that shows a clear vision of what the organisation wants to establish and what will be the basis for the development of the relationship engagement model, the establishment of the transition and change process and the establishment of the relationship management with expectations around all three lines of operation.

The format of this blueprint will vary, as will the level of detail, but typical areas to be included are:

- Expected future state such as the cost base, services being delivered, infrastructure/assets employed, people/culture, relationships, contracts and risks;

- Pricing models including areas where prices may be variable of fixed and the logic behind those models;

- Balanced scorecard model;

- Draft contractual terms;

- The organisation structure that will be retained;

- Governance model;

- Competencies;

- Sourcing strategy.

As part of the blueprint you need to set out the processes for knowledge management and learning. Outsourcing by definition involves some knowledge transfer and it is essential to know how you are going to manage that transfer, understand the level of knowledge being retained in the organisation and understand the learning process to "fill in the gaps". If this is not done properly then knowledge can be lost with the subsequent impact on the delivery of the service. The blueprint for knowledge works both ways, ensuring the supplier has the knowledge to deliver the service and that the client either retains or has access to the knowledge that they require in order to manage the service and to not be entirely reliant on the supplier.

This knowledge management can, and probably should, be enshrined in the contract but it is also true that both sides should realise that knowledge sharing can make basic good sense for both of them.

The blueprint will also include some element of first-draft project management. At what stage will services be shifted across? This is an area that requires some thought as the order in which things are moved to or between suppliers is as important as the timing of those moves.

1.8   UNDERTAKE RISK ASSESSMENT

This is part of setting out the blueprint and involves an initial risk assessment. The NOA Life Cycle suggests a number of areas to cover:

- Financial (both P&L and balance sheet);

- Service delivery;

- Supply;

- Data security;

- Business continuity and disaster recovery;

- Reputational risk and ethical issues;

- Strategic capability (core competency, innovation, knowledge, skills, culture, IPR);

- Legal;

- People;

- Political;

- Relationships.

1.9   DEVELOP AND AGREE BUSINESS CASE

As is usual in business the strategies need to be underpinned by business cases. As highlighted in earlier chapters there are many factors behind the decision to outsource, under the headings of technology, strategy, human and financial. Some of these factors will feed into the specific business case for the organisation looking at its outsourcing strategy. Very often cost is a major factor but it is very rarely the only one and all factors need due consideration in the business case. The key should be overall value rather than any narrow concentration on costs.

The business case requires buy in and support from all key stakeholders. This is an opportunity for the business reasons behind the outsourcing strategy to be challenged.

1.10   CONFIRM AND COMMIT TO GOVERNANCE MODEL

In the previous stages the governance model has been looked at and reviewed but once the business case has been agreed there is an ideal opportunity to revalidate the governance. We are getting to the point where actions are taken to implement the strategy and the organisation starts to make long-term commitments. In the case of personnel this is an opportunity to look at succession planning.

1.11   EXECUTE AND DRIVE STRATEGIES THROUGH LIFE CYCLE

Now the decision process has reached this point it is time to start to engage with suppliers and start the relationship engagement phase. However, one of the most important parts of the NOA Life Cycle framework is that it loops back through the strategic leadership phase throughout. This isn't the end of this phase so it is important that the feedback loops are maintained to ensure that the strategic focus is kept aligned with the overall strategy of the organisation. It is also important that there remains visible leadership to help continue the motivation and dynamism, to deliver continuous improvement, to deliver greater value, and that the relationships between the parties continues to function effectively.

Relationship Engagement Phase

Potential problems

- Incompetent or inappropriate partner selected;

- Inadequate contract agreed;

- Relationship undermined by the selection process;

- No partner identified;

- Procurement process too time consuming and/or costly;

- Potential partners withdraw from the process or not recruited into the process.

Key competency areas

- Managing tender process;

- Reviewing and challenging proposals;

- Conducting due diligence;

- Contract negotiation;

- Business case review;

- Strategic decision making;

- Cultural matching.

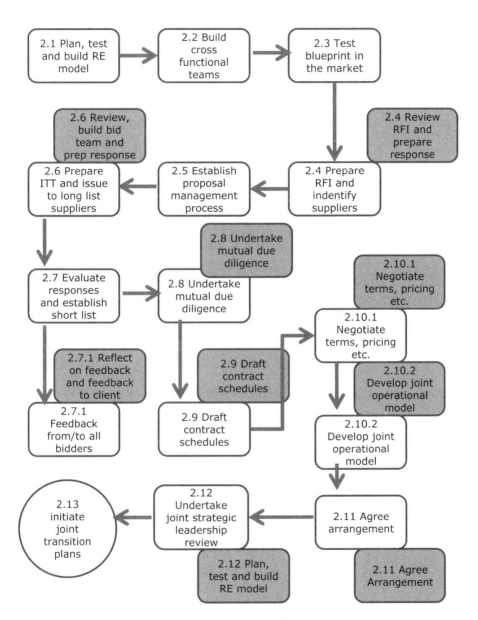

Figure 10.5 The Relationship Engagement Phase

The relationship engagement phase is split in the diagram (Figure 10.5) to show client activities (clear background), supplier activities (dark background).

2.1   PLAN, TEST AND BUILD RELATIONSHIP ENGAGEMENT MODEL

This sets out the relationship engagement model including the scope of services to be outsourced, how that supply chain works (either single or multiple), the criteria and constraints for dealing with suppliers and the overall procurement approach.

2.2   BUILD CROSS-FUNCTIONAL TEAMS

The next part is to put together the relationship management team including how it will work, as well as who is on it. The important thing is to get a wide spread of skills and experience but make sure that those skills and experience are relevant to the service being outsourced so as not to confuse the process and waste valuable time. However, where the Life Cycle refers to 'relevant', you have to take into account future requirements rather than just those for the initial stage.

This may be on a part-time basis but as outsourcing grows and the number of suppliers grows these may become full-time roles.

The NOA Life Cycle recommends people from disciplines such as:

- Technical;

- Operations;

- Contract/legal;

- Finance.

The technical team works on specification of the services. They help suppliers work out if they can deliver the service and if there is sufficient detail to be able to price the service. This will include details of existing hardware and software systems, networks and communications, systems maps and technical strategies. They will also detail out disaster recovery and resilience systems.

The technical team will move on to assess the technical side of the bids that are received and determine their fit with requirements and future strategy.

The operations team provides the operational information for suppliers to properly specify and price their bids. This may include availability requirements, response times, hours of service, acceptable downtime, problem categorisation and expected response times, change request turnaround times and operational dependencies and how operations work together. It is important that the operational information is business-orientated rather than a list of technical output measures. The business-orientated metrics should impact on the business goals of the organisation rather than the more narrow set of technical output specifications which relate to the targets that the service needs to meet to be compliant. Setting these metrics does require a wider consultation within the client organisation, and so takes a lot more effort and time, but not only does it ensure the tender specifications are aligned with the business goals but, by involving a wider audience within the client organisation, gets greater stakeholder buy in.

The operations team should document all this and provide operational, as opposed to technical, process maps and disaster recovery processes.

As with the technical team the operations team will move on to assess the operational side of the bids that are received and determine their fit with requirements and future strategy.

The contract and legal team develop the legal terms and conditions of the supply of the service including the schedules. Most commercial contracts have fairly set legal terms and conditions (although these can be varied given the scope and size of the agreement) plus flexible schedules that are referred to in the legal terms but are mostly different for each agreement. These schedules will specify price, service levels, risk/reward structures, change control process, the service described and defined, disaster recovery process, exit management process, hours of operation, governance, etc. Many of these schedules may not be completed at this stage as they will come about through the tenders and the subsequent contract negotiation, but it is important to make clear at this stage what areas the client expects to be covered in the contract.

As a matter of principle I like to make sure that a draft contract is issued with the tender for comment and is not left for future negotiation.

Not only does this save time later but it also ensures that suppliers are bidding on the same basis. It also gives an idea of the cultural fit of the supplier. When they ask for changes to the standard terms are they asking the sort of things you would ask or are they being overly bureaucratic or too far the other way and being *laissez-faire* with the contract terms. On principle at National Rail Enquiries we only accept the supplier terms in exceptional circumstances.

However contracts do need to be clear and as simple as is possible. At some point in the future someone not involved in the original process may need to pick up the contract to resolve a dispute. This is made all the easier if the contract is clearly written.

The financial team will look at suitable pricing structures, risk allocation, indexation, contract duration and the balance that this needs between cost, security and flexibility. They will also look at the treatment of set-up costs, asset purchases and treatment of existing assets. They should be looking at financial structuring to explore the P&L, tax, balance-sheet and cash-flow impact of various charging and funding models.

The financial team will also need to consider the impact of disclosing the current costs of the operation. This can help suppliers in the bid/no bid decision and can help them understand the scope better. However it can also lead to a cost-centric bid, which may not be what the client wants, and may also lead to a bid that hasn't been fully considered but is just put in as less than the current price in order to secure the service and then worry about the costs later.

Because we have so many suppliers and so many different services at National Rail Enquiries this team take up a large part of the organisation with rail experts, legal, operational, technical, commercial and finance as well as project management experts.

For us this isn't a one-off process and this part of the Life Cycle is continually evolving with tweaks to legal terms and additional work on pricing structures that reflect the reality of the risk. One thing that has been constant is the rate of increase in our engagement with potential suppliers. It is becoming more and more important to engage with suppliers at this stage as the number of suppliers grows but also as the services provided become more diverse and further away from our core areas of expertise.

In each case we use the engagement process not just to help the supplier understand the requirements but also to understand what the suppliers can deliver. It is not uncommon for us to change the specification of what we want during this process as we learn more about what can be done.

2.3 TEST BLUEPRINT IN THE MARKET

Back in the strategic leadership phase there will have been decisions, or at least definite discussions, on how many suppliers it is prudent to obtain bids from, the attitude to consortium and subcontracting, single-source or multi-source, preferred location, if any, and linguistic capabilities if relevant.

These will have fed into the blueprint but that blueprint needs to be tested in the market. This means discussions with potential suppliers to test the viability of what the client wants delivered through this blueprint. This will involve some background checking to avoid suppliers saying that they can deliver only for you to, unwittingly, get the first version of a service with all the risks that entails. Conversely suppliers may wish to put problems in the way of the blueprint in order to steer you to their preferred service. Neither are good and both need checking in the market, and possibly references from other clients, to ensure the client has an understanding of the suitability of the blueprint to the market.

2.4 PREPARE REQUEST FOR INFORMATION (RFI) AND IDENTIFY QUALIFIED SUPPLIERS (SUPPLIERS: REVIEW RFI AND PREPARE RESPONSE)

To a large extent this depends on the service and the maturity of the market. Very often qualified suppliers are well known and can be approached directly (as National Rail Enquiries found when we tendered for cloud hosting services). Sometimes the client may be new to the market and the service less well known or defined and the client will need to seek other means to identify qualified suppliers.

Very often the method for finding suppliers is to issue a Request for Information (RFI). This will include a description of the client and the client's business, an outline of the services required, draft timelines, an indication of the type of supplier wanted and possibly some specific information such as draft pricing. This can be posted in journals and with tender services to get the maximum coverage.

The responses to the RFI can be used to validate the blueprint and to create a long list of suppliers to send the Request for Proposal (RFP) or tender documents to.

For the supplier this is an early chance to see if the opportunity is suitable for them before they have committed much resource on it.

2.5   ESTABLISH PROPOSAL MANAGEMENT PROCESS

One of the first decisions to be made is how many suppliers are to be invited to tender. Too few and you are limiting your options. Too many and you are increasing the workload of assessing the tenders. The process of assessing and communicating with suppliers should not be underestimated. It is a process that requires effort and resource.

As part of this process the client needs to decide who will handle the assessment of the tenders and any questions that the suppliers may ask. Usually the answers to questions are circulated to all tenderers to ensure everyone is bidding on the same basis. However the handling of these questions requires a process and resource.

This process needs to be handled well to keep the tender process on time and to create a feeling of professionalism with the suppliers.

2.6   PREPARE INVITATION TO TENDER (ITT)/REQUEST FOR PROPOSAL (RFP) AND ISSUE TO LONG LIST OF SUPPLIERS (SUPPLIERS: REVIEW, BUILD BID TEAM AND PREPARE RESPONSE)

The tender document then needs to be prepared so that it can be issued to the potential suppliers. Whilst not wanting the document to be too long, it does need to be comprehensive in order to make sure that the tenders are accurate and complete and that the requirements are fully understood. It also needs to ensure a smooth process and timing.

What is included in the ITT varies but general headings would include:

- The procedure to follow for responses including timing, format, address for response and any limitations;

- Information on the client;

- Approach to innovation;

- Information required on the supplier;

- Description of the service and components of the service;

- Service levels and bonus/penalty regime;

- Pricing structure;

- Expectations on indexation;

- Governance structure;

- Treatment of assets;

- Intellectual property treatment;

- Draft contract for responses;

- Staff transfers and details of how legislation such as TUPE will apply;

- Green credentials;

- References.

The construction of the ITT gives the opportunity for a further review of the decision. At this stage very often new ideas are introduced as the discipline of putting together the document forces people to think more deeply on how things will work in operation.

The tender can have a mixture of open and closed questions. Open when you want to explore more about the knowledge and intentions of the supplier and closed when you need answers that are directly comparable.

From the supplier's point of view this is time for the bid/no bid decision. Putting a tender together is not a cheap exercise so suppliers need to make sure they really want to bid before they do. Their decision will be around a number of factors:

- The supplier has to realistically look at their ability to deliver. There is no point in bidding for something if you don't think you can deliver;

- They also have to look at their resourcing for the bid. Sometimes bids come at the same time and decisions need to be made which ones to go for if there aren't enough resources to bid for all of them effectively. It is better to bid for a small number of jobs well than a large number poorly;

- It has to look at whether the service fits with an overall strategy;

- The supplier also needs to look at their fit with the client. It is also a long-term relationship for them so the fit needs to be both ways;

- The supplier should look at the future potential for the service. Can it be expanded or does it have additional benefits such as expending the supplier's range of skills?

- Finally the supplier needs to look at the chance of success. Putting in a tender is like placing a bet. There is a significant investment in bidding, both in terms of cost and lost opportunities elsewhere. If the supplier wins the tender then it will have a financial benefit. The supplier needs to balance the cost and benefit with the probability of success. This depends on the supplier capabilities, its incumbent strengths and the strengths of other bidders.

2.7   EVALUATE RESPONSES AND ESTABLISH SHORTLIST

The client will already have set the criteria for assessing the tenders and now it has to apply those criteria and establish a shortlist. The client will want to compare like for like so there is an opportunity to seek clarification before going into the full assessment.

How much effort is involved at this stage depends on the complexity of the service and its importance to the client organisation. Unsurprisingly, the more important and complex it is the more effort you should put into assessing the tenders.

The assessment needs to be done by experts, which often means breaking parts of it up for different assessors. However the client also needs to be careful to avoid personal bias in the assessment. Where possible team or cross marking helps to reduce the risk of bias.

Typical evaluation areas are:

- Capability and quality;

- Commercial terms;

- Cost effectiveness and cost efficiency;

- Cultural fit;

- People;

- Style of work.

The weighting of these is very important and will depend on the service being tendered. If it is a simple service without much strategic impact and the prime driver is cost then the commercial terms will weigh heaviest. For more strategic services the cultural fit (in National Rail Enquiries we use "like, trust, believe") will weigh heavier.

However this is done the final result is a shortlist of suppliers who can fulfil the requirements at an economic price. The shortlist does need to be short (we normally only have two) as the amount of effort to do the final evaluation and negotiation is considerable. However I wouldn't advise going to one at this stage as there is a need for some competitive tension when working on these final issues.

2.7.1   FEEDBACK FROM/TO ALL BIDDERS
(SUPPLIERS: REFLECT ON FEEDBACK AND FEEDBACK TO CLIENT)

The client will give feedback to the suppliers at this stage and the suppliers need to take this seriously and learn from the comments. The unsuccessful suppliers will learn to improve future bids and those on the shortlist will learn more to help them in the final stages.

It is also useful if, following this, the client gets feedback from the suppliers. Things may not have been clear in the ITT and tender process and it is useful to know this for future reference. After a tender, whether successful or unsuccessful, everyone needs to learn to do better next time.

2.8   UNDERTAKE MUTUAL DUE DILIGENCE/TEST CULTURAL FIT (CLIENT AND SUPPLIER)

This is a mutual due diligence exploring more deeply both the understanding of the service and what the supplier can offer but also the cultures of the two organisations and their fit together. Both sides need to be comfortable that they can build a long-term relationship as well as being comfortable that they understand the service required and the service being offered.

This stage involves significant contact between the client organisation and the suppliers on the shortlist. This contact will be at various levels and will involve the sharing of information. All this helps increase the confidence on both sides and also helps the client organisation with their final decision on which supplier to go with.

This phase is an opportunity for the supplier to evaluate the existing staff both for the management of the future contract and for staff who will be involved in the delivery and possibly transferred over to the supplier.

Another area to cover is the exit strategy. It seems strange to talk about exit before you have even selected the supplier, but this isn't just for the final exit from the agreement not yet signed, it also covers the exit from the incumbent or the exit from the in-house operation. As strange as it may seem, it is easier to talk about this now than it is once the final selection has been made.

There will be a tendency on both sides to get the deal done and get on with delivering the service. However the phrase "marry in haste, repent at leisure" works in outsourcing (there are quite a few comparisons you can make between outsourcing and marriage). It is a good idea to take time over this phase and make sure the final decision is right for both parties.

2.9   DRAFT CONTRACT SCHEDULES (CLIENT AND SUPPLIER)

The client needs firstly to discuss any changes the supplier has requested in the draft contract that was sent out. The requested changes need to be discussed and agreed as the client needs to weigh any changes the supplier insists on in the evaluation of the final decision.

Also at this stage the contract schedules need to start to be populated.

The schedules are really the heart of the contract. These detail out what is going to be done, charging structures and bonus/penalty arrangements etc. The schedules are far more likely to be referred to in the future than the legal T&Cs. If you are looking at the legal T&Cs later on then something has gone wrong. Getting the schedules right and agreed is so important for the future service.

2.10.1 NEGOTIATE TERMS, PRICING, MI AND JOINT GOVERNANCE (CLIENT AND SUPPLIER)

Despite the thoroughness of the tender process there will still be some negotiation to do on the terms of the agreement mainly because the due diligence very often brings out changes which may be requested by either side.

The client can also clear up the final strings of the governance structure at this time.

It is also a chance for the client to call for "best and final offers" from the shortlist. You can negotiate for years if you want but at some point you have to say what the final price is going to be and both sides need to accept this as final. The client can then close the tender as far as cost is concerned.

This phase needs to be completed in a collaborative way. If things cannot be resolved amicably at this point then you have to question how it will work during the contract.

2.10.2 DEVELOP JOINT OPERATIONAL MODEL AND TRANSITION/ EXIT PLANS (CLIENT AND SUPPLIER)

The exit and transition plans are finalised, as is the ongoing operational model. The exit and transition plans are completed in the schedules together with a clear understanding of who is paying for what in those plans.

2.11 AGREE ARRANGEMENT (CLIENT AND SUPPLIER)

There then needs to be a final check back to the overall business strategies for the client and the supplier and, provided this is still fine, there can be formal sign off of the decision. The supplier can be selected and the contract finalised and signed.

2.12   UNDERTAKE JOINT STRATEGIC LEADERSHIP REVIEW AND AGREE ACTIONS (SUPPLIERS: PLAN, TEST AND BUILD RE MODEL)

Now the decision has been made there can be a joint learning review to critique the process and learn for future tenders as well as learning what can be done better in the new arrangement and support the development of that arrangement.

2.13   INITIATE JOINT TRANSITION PLANS/EXIT PLANS

The client, with the help of the supplier, now needs to manage the transition from the Relationship Engagement phase to the Transition and Change phase. At this point some people, both on the client and supplier side, may leave the process so the knowledge management process needs to make sure their knowledge is captured and not lost to the ongoing service. It is difficult for the people who are charged with transitioning the service to be able to do this in the optimum way if they have either lost or don't have access to the knowledge built up during the earlier stages.

Transition and Change Phase

POTENTIAL PROBLEMS

- Delays in go live;

- Stakeholder requirements not addressed fully or effectively;

- De-motivated team;

- Knowledge lost;

- Knowledge corrupted;

- Assets lost and/or not fully recovered;

- Data integrity poor or data lost;

- Poor systems performance;

- Poor environment affecting performance;

- Legal issues and legal costs;

- Confusion between old and new processes;

- Disaffected exiting providers.

KEY COMPETENCY AREAS

- Project management;

- Process design;

- Transformation design and management;

- HR management;

- Data migration and configuration;

- Acceptance testing;

- Training;

- Facilities management;

- Transition and exit planning;

- Communication;

- Novation;

- Knowledge management and transfer;

- Process shadowing;

- Facility decommissioning;

- Asset recovery;

- Financial management and control.

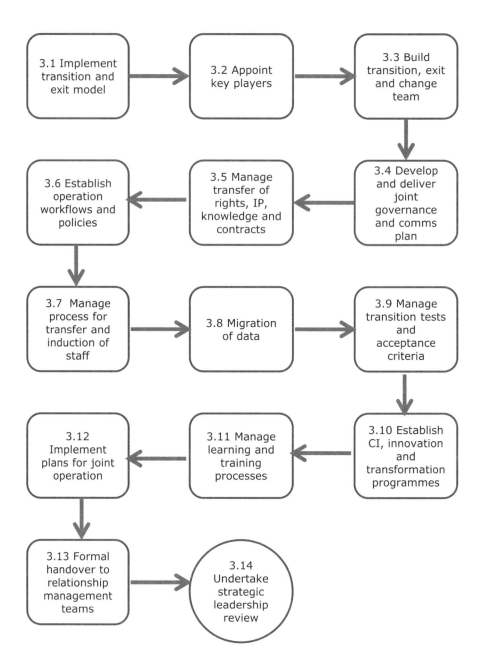

Figure 10.6   The Transition and Change Phase

3.1   IMPLEMENT TRANSITION AND EXIT MODEL

The contract has been agreed and the transition can now begin, underpinned by the work done during the relationship engagement phase.

3.2   APPOINT KEY PLAYERS

At this point the key players for programme and project management are appointed by both sides and can then start working together on the transition. They will also have other key players in the transition team appointed but they bear the day-to-day responsibility for the overall transition project.

3.3   BUILD TRANSITION, EXIT AND CHANGE TEAM AND OPERATIONAL ENVIRONMENT

Following on from the appointment of the programme and project managers, both the client and supplier need to build up the transition team around them. These should already be selected and ready to be put into place through the Relationship Engagement phase but now they need to be put into place and committed to the project.

The skill set required at transition is different from the engagement stage but it is useful to have as much continuity as possible, even if it is just for the early stages until the transition has made some progress.

Depending on the service being transitioned there is usually a requirement for project and programme management skills, technical expertise, operational expertise, contract and financial expertise as well as conflict resolution skills (normally part of the project and programme management skills but sometimes a specialist is required to step in).

The technical teams will work on the current infrastructure, the proposed infrastructure and the plan to move from the former to the latter. This will involve project planning and risk analysis together with roll back and disaster recovery plans in case stages don't work. The idea is to make the transition with no interference on business as usual but, if this is not possible, at least to minimise the interference.

Operational teams will similarly look at the existing processes and the proposed processes and see how to move from one to the other with minimal disruption. They will have to deal with staff transfers, any redundancies and change management through the process.

The involvement of contract and finance skills should hopefully be embodied in the programme and project management skills. These people will be aware of the contract timescales and costs for transition and the service to be delivered through and after the transition. It is their responsibility to monitor the timescales and costs and also adherence to the project plan so that the services are delivered as per the contract and in the timing of the contract. They need to manage any issues that may arise around these targets but should not be afraid to call in contract or financial expertise if it is needed.

The supplier may have teams with lengthy experience on this form of transition and the client may not, or they may be equally experienced. It is becoming more common for the client team to be more experienced than the supplier with some clients embracing outsourcing as a normal way of conducting business. This was noticeable when I worked in the oil industry where outsourcing of key functions, such as the seismic surveying, has been standard practice for years. However regardless of the relative experience this is a joint process where collaboration will benefit both parties.

3.4   DEVELOP, DELIVER AND MAINTAIN JOINT GOVERNANCE AND INTERNAL COMMUNICATIONS PLAN

The transition team is also responsible for the joint governance and internal communications of the project at this stage. These can use various methodologies and tools from electronic notice boards, blogs and websites through to town hall meetings and one-to-one or small group sessions. They are all valid and all have their place but they also all have different uses, and one of the skills of governance is to pick the right communication tools for the right communications.

Communication is key to governance and even which communication method is to be used in any given situation needs to be communicated.

The communication needs to be two way and ensure escalation within the governance structure. Questions raised and input required need to be dealt with at the appropriate level and with the appropriate skill set and the communication process needs to assist this and make sure it gets to the right people as quickly as possible.

It is difficult to underestimate the importance of communication in good governance and to underestimate the importance of good governance in successful outsourcing. It is key to success in outsourcing.

3.5 MANAGE TRANSFER OF RIGHTS/OWNERSHIP OF INTELLECTUAL PROPERTY RIGHTS (IPR), OPERATIONAL KNOWLEDGE AND THIRD-PARTY CONTRACTS

It should be the case that this is just implementing what has been decided and documented in the Relationship Engagement phase. However in practice it is not unusual for new information to come to light which changes what was agreed at the Relationship Engagement phase.

One of the biggest issues to face is how to deal with changes at this stage. The supplier may wish to change pricing and the client may wish to reject this on the basis that the supplier has done its due diligence and should have discovered any variances. Being at different ends of the scale can undermine much of the relationship work that has been done to date so it is important that these issues are approached in a constructive and positive manner.

This is one of the first areas to truly test the cultural fit of the two organisations and allows both sides to see whether their impression of cultural fit is correct. It is important that a mutually acceptable solution is reached in any issues at this stage.

3.6 ESTABLISH OPERATIONS WORKFLOWS AND SUPPORTING POLICIES

As with 3.5, this should merely be implementing what has been discussed and agreed at the Relationship Engagement phase. However, as with 3.5 it is possible that new information will come to light changing the already agreed processes and policies.

This is also an important test of the relationship and cultural fit and both sides need to approach any changes in a positive way.

3.7   MANAGE PROCESS FOR TRANSFER AND INDUCTION OF STAFF

This is obviously a key area for legal reasons but it is also important that this is managed well for the staff. You are transferring assets but human assets need to be handled with a lot more tact and care than physical and IP assets.

Induction and training may be required, but these should be done with a tone and approach that realises that these are people, and they are people in an uncertain situation with all the stresses that go along with that uncertainty.

Get this wrong and it could take a long time to recover.

3.8   MIGRATION OF DATA

The supplier should have experience and tried and tested procedures for managing this. During the Relationship Engagement phase they will have looked at the data and its format and worked out how to migrate it into the new system. They may even have tested sample data into the new system.

This is an essential phase but should be straightforward. If you can't get this right then something went wrong earlier in the process.

3.9   MANAGE TRANSITION TESTS AND ACCEPTANCE CRITERIA

Again the supplier should have tried and tested procedures for this and, in this case, the tests are probably enshrined in the contract.

Transition and acceptance tests are complex and can sometimes be failed but there should be no doubts about how the tests work and what constitutes success or failure.

3.10   ESTABLISH INNOVATION AND TRANSFORMATION PROGRAMMES

These programmes need to be established to ensure the new service does not stagnate. They would have been discussed at the Relationship Engagement phase and now have to be properly established to ensure the desired culture is there and working.

3.11   MANAGE LEARNING AND TRAINING PROCESSES

Staff need to be fully competent with the service being delivered, and the training and learning processes set up at the Relationship Engagement phase now needs to be implemented and managed to ensure the service delivers the benefit it was planned to.

Very often failed acceptance is down to inadequate staff learning or training.

However this isn't just for the transition, it is also for the ongoing running of the service.

3.12   IMPLEMENT PLANS FOR JOINT OPERATION DURING AND AFTER TRANSITION

The actual cutover is a very nervous time for everyone involved. Sometimes there is a period of joint operation or parallel running before final cutover. Sometimes this is essential for disaster recovery.

The whole area of cost, duration and acceptance for final cutover will have been discussed and agreed at the Relationship Engagement phase but you must be prepared to be flexible. It is no use sticking to the plan if the plan isn't going to work.

3.13   FORMAL HANDOVER TO RELATIONSHIP MANAGEMENT AND OPERATIONS TEAMS

This point is based around the cutover but it shouldn't be like flicking a switch. There is as much a need for retained knowledge here as there was in the handover from Relationship Engagement to the Transition and Change process.

There needs to be a definite time when responsibilities move over but that doesn't mean that the previous team walks away. There is nearly always a need to rely on the experience and knowledge of those who have gone before you.

The overall Strategic Leadership needs to ensure that this handover of knowledge happens and that there are opportunities to explore the experience already gained during the process.

3.14   UNDERTAKE STRATEGIC LEADERSHIP LEARNING REVIEW AND AGREE ACTIONS

This is another point for the lessons learned exercise. Ideally this will all have gone 100 per cent smoothly but it usually doesn't and there is always something to be learnt from what went right and what didn't go right.

Relationship Management Phase

POTENTIAL PROBLEMS

- Adversarial relationship creating tensions;

- Poor teamwork;

- Culture clash;

- Process stagnation;

- Inefficient change control;

- Budget overruns;

- Poor performance;

- Low staff morale;

- High staff turnover;

- Service levels poor;

- Contract deliverables not achieved;

- Change control causing confusion and impacting on agreed contract;

- Stakeholder needs not met.

KEY COMPETENCY AREAS

- Programme leadership and management;

- Learning and development management and delivery;

- Cultural development management;

- Conflict management;

- Negotiation;

- Communication;

- Benchmarking;

- Process improvement management;

- Financial management and control;

- Team building;

- Risk management.

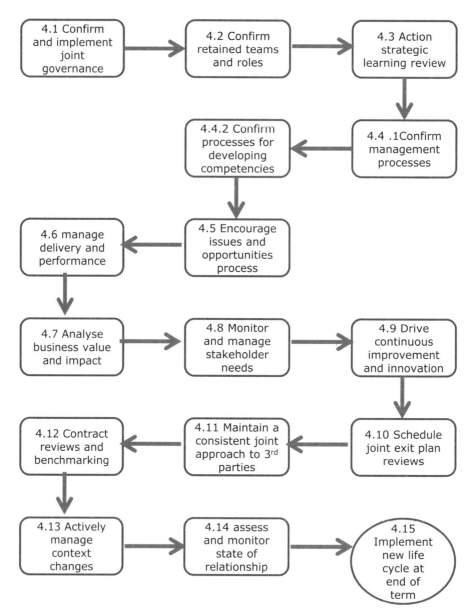

Figure 10.7   The Relationship Management Phase

4.1   CONFIRM AND IMPLEMENT ONGOING JOINT GOVERNANCE MODEL ALIGNED TO STRATEGIC VALUE

The joint governance model is at the heart of successful outsourcing relationship management but the level of governance is dependent on the strategic importance of the relationship. You would not expect an oil company to put the same level of governance into the agreement for the cleaning of their offices as they would with the agreement to drill and test the oil wells.

The more strategically important the relationship the more effort will be put into the governance.

The balance that needs to be met between the client and supplier should have been resolved at the Relationship Engagement phase but it is still important to see if they are still aligned. Issues may arise if the perception of the importance of the relationship is different and so one side does not commit the resource that the other would expect.

A typical joint governance model will have strategic, management and operational levels. The frequency and content of the meetings at the various levels will differ naturally but they will also differ across agreements. Again this reflects the strategic importance of the relationship and the more important it is the more frequent the more senior meetings are likely to be.

Running parallel to the joint governance is the organisation's own governance processes. Not everything will be discussed openly and some things need to be discussed solely within the client or supplier organisations. What comes out of the internal governance meetings may be shared at a joint level but there is still a need for internal governance discussions.

4.2   CONFIRM RETAINED TEAMS AND ROLES

This refers to the staff retained within the client organisation. This will ensure that key knowledge is retained and that the client retains the skills to properly monitor the supplier and their running of the service.

There is a cost to a retained team so the normal cost benefit comparisons will apply. Too many people in the retained team and the benefits of outsourcing could be negated. Too few and you run the risk of not being able to effectively run your outsourcing operation.

It is essential that each role is therefore considered carefully and whilst there may have been agreement on the make-up of these teams earlier in the process things do change, so a review should be made.

4.3   ACTION STRATEGIC LEADERSHIP LEARNING REVIEW – REGULARLY CONFIRM VALUES AND DRIVERS

Once the transition is completed a review needs to be completed to see what has been learnt. This should be undertaken by both sides, as by now they will have been working together for a period of time and the reflection is important for the ongoing relationship.

This review should be as open as possible and will help to identify future opportunities as well as problems. This is an ongoing process that will confirm the status of the relationship and help to keep strategy and values aligned.

4.4.1   CONFIRM CONTRACT/SERVICE/CHANGE MANAGEMENT PROCESSES

The contract management, service management and change management processes will have been described earlier in the process. However an outsourcing agreement is a developing process and these things should be reviewed and make sure they are still agreed, appropriate and working.

This area includes:

- Project changes;

- Changes to the contract;

- SLAs and whether they are being met;

- Forecasts and projections;

- A reference back to the business case;

- Documentation processes;

- IP issues;

- Feedback from stakeholders and third parties;

- Disputes;

- Suggested changes to the future service;

- Possible personnel changes.

4.4.2 CONFIRM PROCESSES FOR DEVELOPING COMPETENCIES AND CULTURE OF OUTSOURCE SERVICE

This should have been agreed earlier in the Life Cycle but it needs to be reviewed and confirmed in the live environment. The client side will need to have input into required skills and knowledge development on the supplier side and any cultural issues that need to be better aligned.

4.5 ENCOURAGE A CANDID, TRUST-BASED ISSUES AND OPPORTUNITIES PROCESS

To try to avoid an adversarial relationship developing you need to encourage a candid trust-based approach. It is easy to slip into such an unsatisfactory relationship but every effort needs to be taken to keep the trust-based approach going, as this will help with focusing on opportunities rather than friction.

4.6 MANAGE DELIVERY AND PERFORMANCE ROBUSTLY – CELEBRATE SUCCESS OFTEN

Performance and service delivery don't just happen. They need to be managed. Systems need to be in place to provide the information to enable this management to take place. You also need to be sure that the people who get the management information are able to analyse that information and identify trends and issues.

To help motivate both the client and supplier staff success should be celebrated. The service delivery is being delivered by the staff of the two organisations so, if it is going well, make sure everyone knows.

4.7 ANALYSE BUSINESS VALUE AND IMPACT

This goes beyond the service levels and agreed performance metrics, and asks the question as to whether the business value and impact of the service can be improved. As has been stated before, an outsourcing agreement is a fluid thing that changes with time. It is important that it doesn't become frozen in time (usually at the time the contract was signed).

An outsourcing arrangement needs to be constantly reviewed to see if it can be improved or it will stagnate, and contract performance metrics are all too often an overly blunt instrument and can become sub-optimal, or even completely ineffective, over time.

4.8   MONITOR, CLARIFY AND MANAGE ALL STAKEHOLDER NEEDS AND PERCEPTIONS

Stakeholder management is of considerable importance to make sure that the needs of the stakeholders are still being met. Not only do you need to ensure that the arrangement still meets the business needs as time passes but to do that you need to keep reviewing what those business needs are.

Achieving this requires good communication and facilitation skills to manage the interface and ensure that the needs are being met and stakeholder perceptions are in line.

4.9   DRIVE MEASUREABLE CONTINUOUS IMPROVEMENT AND INNOVATION

One of the advantages of outsourcing is the skills and experience the supplier can bring in from other areas outside of the client relationship. You need to be able to drive the agreement to be able to get the full benefit of that advantage.

The measurement of continuous improvement and innovation will help to achieve the benefit to the client organisation.

4.10   SCHEDULE JOINT EXIT PLAN REVIEWS TO ENSURE THEY ARE CURRENT

Discussing the exit plan during the operation of the service can be uncomfortable. However, like everything in the agreement, the exit plan may change with time and it needs to be kept updated to minimise problems that may occur at exit.

The client will feel more comfortable with an up-to-date exit plan and, from a supplier point of view, having an effective exit plan doesn't make it more likely that the client will avail themselves of it.

4.11   MAINTAIN A CONSISTENT JOINT APPROACH WITH THIRD PARTIES

As an outsourcing arrangement is mostly a partnership the partners need to ensure they have a consistent outward position. They must be seen as one and the same.

4.12   CONTRACT REVIEWS AND BENCHMARKING

There is usually provision in the contract for reviews of the contract and benchmarking against the market (usually on price). This needs to be done but you should consider joint benchmarking in areas such as technology to ensure that the service is not just at a good price but also up to date.

4.13   ACTIVELY MANAGE CONTEXT CHANGES

This is one of the key ongoing functions. Things will change and, whilst you should make the contract reflect this as far as possible, this very often comes down to the relationship, negotiation and an understanding of each party's strategic drivers.

However you should bear in mind that sometimes these changes cannot be met and either complete or partial exit from the contract may be necessary. In this case managing the relationship is even more important to ensure a smooth exit.

4.14   ASSESS AND MONITOR STATE OF THE RELATIONSHIP ROUTINELY

At some levels an outsourcing arrangement can just be a list of performance metrics and service levels and as long as these are met the relationship is fine. This is usually for routine services that are not close to the core business of the client.

However more important services usually go beyond the contractual requirements and the service will change and develop as time goes on.

It is in these arrangements that the ongoing monitoring of the state of the relationship is so important. If the relationship is healthy changes can be easier to agree and implement and the development of the service can continue.

The state of the relationship will also impact on the ability to resolve issues that arise during the agreement.

It is important that there are systems in place to monitor the state of the relationship, and one of these can be a third-party survey undertaken on the attitudes of the client or the supplier towards the relationship and the other party.

4.15   IMPLEMENT NEW LIFE CYCLE PROCESS AT END OF TERM

Whether the decision at term end is to renew, bring back in-house or retender, the implementation of the new Life Cycle cannot be left until the end. Starting this before the end date will make the transition smoother, and even in the case of a renewal the process will be smoother with a Life Cycle approach being started prior to the end date.

Summary

At first reading the framework may seem at the same time to be a significant amount of work and may be also seem to be over-simplifying a very complex set of relationships. However, a systematic approach to outsourcing can lead to significant benefits and the framework needs to be adapted to take into account the significance of the service in the client's strategy. It is also only a framework and the level of complexity needs to be assessed by the client and the supplier in their approach to this framework. Outsourcing governance is complex and is becoming more so (Martorelli 2011) but that means a more structured approach rather than pulling away from the governance.

You will also find that the Life Cycle sounds more time consuming written down than it does in practice. With the right skill set in place and the right resource many of the processes above are second nature and much of the complexity is dealt with through expertise rather than excessive resource.

As mentioned several time in this book governance in an essential part of outsourcing. It is believed that as much as 15–20 per cent of the value of an outsourcing contract can be lost through a lack of governance (Lepeak, Beals, Campbell and Moore 2011).

It is important that there is a process behind managing an outsourcing relationship and the National Outsourcing Association's outsourcing Life Cycle is a well-researched starting point but it isn't a fixed process to be followed. It is a guide.

Chapter 11

Minimising the Downside and Maximising the Upside

I believe there are many situations where outsourcing can be beneficial to a client organisation. However, you need to make sure that it is beneficial to your company and that it fits with your overall strategy. You also need to set up some form of governance process, with the National Outsourcing Association's Life Cycle, as discussed in the previous chapter, offering some possible guidance on what to do and when to do it.

However there are other mechanisms to help the client make the best of an outsourcing arrangement. Some of these apply more to some outsourcing models than others but in general they are all worth considering. As with most of the sections in this book I caveat these mechanisms in that they may not be suitable, practical or even possible in all situations, so you need to exercise some judgement.

a)   One of the mechanisms we used in National Rail Enquiries is to avoid long contract commitments but to also leave the contracts with plenty of room for rolling extensions. That gives a natural break if the service isn't going well but allows you to run it on if it is. The comments people make on this mechanism are usually:

  • "You don't need a short term because if it isn't running well you should be able to terminate under failure by the supplier."

That would be true if a contract could include every foreseeable problem. However it can't. Sometimes a supplier can be meeting every contractual requirement but really isn't delivering what you want. Another possibility is that the requirements have changed and the service levels in the contract, whilst being met, aren't what the service now needs. A short commitment gives the client an exit without the need for the supplier to be in breach.

- "A short-term commitment doesn't motivate the supplier to invest in the service".

My experience has proven to be contrary to this. The rolling extensions can be seen as giving the supplier a very long contract if they are able to keep the client happy. A long fixed-term contract gives the supplier the security but, to a certain extent, removes the drive to excel in the role as they have a fixed term in the bag. They just need to meet the SLAs.

In the catering company Gardner Merchant we didn't like long-term or any type of fixed-term contract and preferred rolling 60-day notice agreements from day one. If a fixed-term contract comes to an end the client is likely to go to tender. Even if you win you tend to lose some margin on a retender but on a rolling contract the client is likely to only think of retendering if your performance is not up to scratch. Gardner Merchant had 60-day notice catering contracts that they had been running for 20 years.

- "A short-term contract will be expensive as the set-up costs have a shorter time to be recovered over".

I will cover this in more detail under the next point but set-up costs should be a separate cost. You are going to pay them whether they are on a one-year or ten-year contract and if they are included in the running costs you risk overpaying if you extend the agreement. The term shouldn't affect the total of the set-up costs but can impact on the lifetime cost if the supplier needs to add in an interest and financing cost for delayed payment.

b)   One of the mechanisms we also use is to get a great deal of transparency of costs in the agreement and to ensure that the costs reflect the cost drivers behind them.

There is no harm in getting the workings behind the costs from the supplier and including those in the contract. It doesn't have to reveal their margins but if you have the details of how the costs are made up you have a much better chance of agreeing changes to those costs if and when the service requirements change.

The pricing should also reflect the drivers behind them. It can be a mistake to force a supplier into bidding a fixed cost for something where the cost drivers are variable. Equally it can be a mistake to have the supplier bid on a variable income where much of their cost base will be fixed. The National Audit Office has detailed an example of this.

In 2011 Capita took on work clamping and confiscating vehicles that did not have road tax on behalf of the Driver and Vehicle Licensing Agency. Unfortunately it took it on under the model of being funded by clamping release charges and the disposal of confiscated vehicles. As it turned out the volume of these fees was not as high as expected and the revenue fell short. After two years Capita had lost £9 million and the Agency terminated the agreement early rather than renegotiate (Morse 2013a).

To show where you can try to align supplier costs with the charging mechanics I can use an example of the National Rail Enquiries call centre contract where the pricing is ultimately simple, but complex in its description. The call centre costs are split into four. Firstly there are the set-up costs which the supplier bid as a fixed price. We expect them to meet this as a fixed price because they should know how much it will cost to set up the call centre to meet the initial volume. We don't want them rolling set-up costs into an ongoing call cost and taking the risk on call volumes, nor do we want them over-recovering if they underestimate the call volumes. We also want to understand their financing costs to see if it is better for us to fund the set-up costs rather than put them onto the supplier.

Next there are certain costs that the supplier can vary but not on a daily basis. Things like floor space, management overhead, training costs, etc. For these costs the supplier bids for call bands on a six-monthly interval. We then forecast calls for those six months and pay them the fixed costs within that band. We don't want the supplier getting stuck with overhead that it can't flex and can't get paid for but we also want them to flex the fixed costs over time to reflect long-term changes in call volumes.

Then comes the variable costs of the service which relates to the actual cost of handling the calls including the costs of the advisor, telecoms etc. – this is a price per call. We expect the supplier to handle the day-to-day operating and staffing of the service and to handle the calls within various parameters.

The final part of the pricing is the penalty and rewards around meeting certain service parameters including external measures such as customer satisfaction.

All these costs are described in some detail so that if, for example, the set-up is delayed through the fault of National Rail Enquiries, we are in a position to be able to agree the revised costs with some knowledge of the logic behind the costs. We also agree things like the average handling time for calls so if that increases, which is usually due to actions by us, the variable cost calculations make it easy to adjust the price.

c)   The allocation of risk needs to be carefully considered. At National Rail Enquiries we adopted the principle that the risk should lie where the control of that risk lies.

In the previous example we structured the call centre pricing to allocate risk to where we think it should lie.

The set-up costs are fixed and the supplier is guaranteed the fixed amount. We do not bear the risk of the supplier overrunning on the set-up costs, and the supplier does not bear the risk of loading the set-up costs into a variable charge. We don't ask the supplier to load fixed costs into a variable rate and take the risk on volumes. National Rail Enquiries has been developing self-service channels which have reduced the call volumes so we take the volume risk. However we do expect the supplier to take the risk on managing the handling of the calls effectively, which is why we don't have an hourly rate.

There are obviously instances where the risk cannot be controlled by either party. In that case the default position is to take the risk on the client side. If you ask a supplier to take a risk on for you they probably will but will charge a risk premium. That risk premium will be higher if the supplier can't control or mitigate the risk so you are picking up the cost anyway.

d)   There needs to be sufficient detail in the service description.

The more detail you have in the schedules of the contract the more clarity you will have. It can be argued that less detail makes the agreement more flexible but in my view that is the road to disputes. If you want flexibility, work on it in the governance and supplier selection rather than by making the requirements vague.

It is also true that a vague service description will make the supplier nervous and cause them to increase their risk margin.

It is important at this stage to understand that I am referring to the outputs of the service rather than how the service is run. You need to know how the service is being run but it is important to keep focused on outputs.

e) Agree an early exit clause under "termination for convenience".

Whilst National Rail Enquiries commit to short terms in their contracts we usually also put in "termination for convenience" clauses. National Rail Enquiries can terminate at any time without cause if there are unforeseen circumstances that may mean the supplier is no longer suitable or the service is either no longer required or is required in a different form that cannot be met under the current arrangement. It is difficult to craft a contract so that every possibility is catered for, so you cannot always rely on contract performance requirements to get a client out of a contract they no longer want.

It is usually fair that such early termination clauses involve a payment to the supplier. They have put the effort in for a certain length of agreement that they now won't get so they deserve some recompense for that. However, from the client's point of view, it is much easier to negotiate a termination for convenience compensation formula at the time of the tender rather than once the supplier has been selected.

The supplier should also not fear such a clause. They will receive recompense for the effort they have put in for the expected term and if the situation arises where the client no longer needs or wants their services a continuing contract is only likely to lead to conflict.

f) At National Rail Enquiries we always tried to make sure that, wherever possible, we owned any intellectual property involved. The principle is that "if we paid for it we own it". If there is IP that is pre-existing we would look for an ongoing licence to use that IP, albeit probably on restricted-use terms.

This helps with the portability of the service. The client can take an existing service and "lift and shift" it to a new supplier. There are issues with the ability of a new supplier to support IP that has not been developed by their own people, so this isn't perfect, but it does allow the client to quickly move a service.

We also encouraged the use of open-source or easily available software which helps the flexibility to move across suppliers.

This is obviously not always possible as sometimes the benefit that a supplier can bring comes from their own proprietary IP that they cannot pass on or even sub-licence.

Whatever the situation, trying to get rights over the systems used is advantageous provided it is possible and provided it doesn't come at too high a cost.

g)   Put the effort in at the tender stage and make sure everyone understands what is required. The effort at this stage pays dividends and is far more effective than trying to fix things later on. It also makes the tender process more valuable as the suppliers have greater support to develop their own understanding. Without this effort you risk excluding an excellent supplier just because you didn't spend the effort for them to fully understand the requirements of the service. Even worse, you risk ending up with a shortlist of suppliers who don't understand the requirements of the service.

It is the old metaphor of building a house. Put the effort in at the beginning to make sure the design is sound and the foundations are properly designed and built and the rest should work. If you don't get the design and foundations right then it is really difficult and expensive to fix it later.

h)   Remember that it probably won't be alright on the night. I have seen instances in my career where the client or supplier gets so far down the road they just want to see the agreement signed. At that stage sometimes there can be a tendency to agree to things and hope it will be OK or at least hope you can fix it later.

I would advise against this. Take the effort and fix it at the time. Blind faith that everything will work can sometimes workout OK, but it is a big risk and one that is unnecessary.

i)   Listen to the suppliers, they may just know what they are talking about. You are bringing in suppliers because of their expertise in the service you are tendering. They may well have advice as to how the service can be delivered better. There is a natural distrust of this as you are likely to feel that the supplier is trying to manipulate the process to their own advantage (which they probably are attempting to do). However, whilst caution is often justified, you should take note of what the suppliers have to say and not dismiss it out of hand.

j)   Resource up for the running of the service. As stated frequently in this book, governance of the ongoing contract is key. To be able to effectively manage that governance you have to have the resource to achieve it. There will be a tendency to try to save money to try to maximise the financial benefit of the outsourcing agreement and, of course, you don't want to waste money. However governance is very important and you need to make sure you have enough people to manage the agreement and that you are not left short in this area.

k)   Make sure you not only have the right number of people to manage the relationship but also the right skill set. Just putting more people on the project isn't the whole answer as they need to have the right skills to manage the outsourcing relationship. It is also often true that people who were good at operating the service when it was in-house are not necessarily the right people to run an outsourcing arrangement.

National Rail Enquiries have changed the nature of their staffing to reflect the need for greater governance, and a different skill set, to cope with multi-sourcing. In the past five years the balance of staff between those with rail expertise and those with outsourcing expertise has moved from over 40 per cent rail to less than 25 per cent. The increase in those with outsourcing skills has been in contract and service management, project management, process management and service delivery with some increase in procurement and business development.

Whilst this may seem an obvious point some thought needs to be applied to the skills that are needed. This will vary according to your outsourcing strategy and how you want to approach it. Your strategy will rule what is run by the client and what is run by the supplier and that rules your skill set requirements.

However it is important, both in the level and skill set of your management, that you don't kid yourself that you are properly geared up for a sophisticated multi-sourcing operation. Have a realistic look and, if possible, get other people to evaluate your management capability before embarking on the multi-sourcing path. If you start with the right set up you will avoid a lot of grief further down the track.

l)   The management of the suppliers needs to be a serious and respected function to get the right people to work for it and to make sure it has the proper authority within the client organisation. The degree you take this to depends on your outsourcing strategy, but wherever you are on the outsourcing barometer, the outsourcing function in the client organisation needs to be in a position of authority and respect. If that isn't the case, if it is seen as a backwater, then it will be harder to attract the right staff and for them to be taken seriously by the supplier. This will hinder the governance process and will lead to sub-optimum results.

m)   The client needs to drive supplier performance. You can't just sit back and hope things will improve. Driving performance from suppliers is much like driving performance from employees. You can try shouting but it usually doesn't work. Working with the supplier and encouraging them to achieve higher performance is usually the best approach. However you are not there to run the business for the supplier. You don't want to build up a mirror organisation on the client side to make up for shortfalls in the supplier performance. If the supplier really isn't working then finding another supplier, however painful that may be, is probably a better solution than upping your governance to a point where you have a mirror organisation.

n)   Use tricks of the trade to get the most out of suppliers. Over the years I have seen and helped to develop various tricks to improve relationships with suppliers and help them and the client organisation understand what each side needs and to help deliver benefit to all.

One of the techniques we used at National Rail Enquiries is to hold six-monthly supplier days. We invite nearly all our suppliers to these, and they normally involve a day of work followed by an evening social event. During the day we run a number of presentations on things such as:

- Our key performance indicators, our current status in achieving them, what our plans are for meeting them and the issues we face;

- Our technology roadmap showing what changes we plan to make and what new technologies we want to introduce. It also covers the timing of these changes;

- A general industry update to give the suppliers some broader background;

- Developments in other parts of National Rail Enquiries, again for background but in this case specific to our business.

The reason for the supplier days and the presentations is very simple. We can't expect suppliers to help us meet our business targets if they don't know what they are. The supplier needs to know what the targets are, the strategic importance of those targets and some of the issues we face meeting them.

With that understanding they are much better placed to use their existing expertise, and the knowledge they gain from their wider exposure to other industries, to help us.

Furthermore, giving them a heads up on our technology roadmap will help them to achieve innovation. Sometimes innovation can come as a sudden flash of light. However in most cases innovation comes through a process of small improvements on existing systems and products. If we share our technology roadmap then the supplier has some guidance to our plans and can focus on helping us achieve innovation along those plans. Their thinking can be more focused.

Also a general background of the industry and National Rail Enquiries helps put what we are trying to do in a wider context. Here the suppliers can be very helpful as we could be as guilty as any for "not seeing the wood for the trees" and suppliers can help with the wider picture.

These supplier days help us but they also help the suppliers. By giving them more information it helps them narrow down their attempts to increase their level of business with us. The understanding they gain can help a more focused approach and help them avoid looking at areas that aren't going to work for us. The more general background can help them see if they can increase their business with us in areas they may never have considered.

An important part of the day is the social event afterwards where the suppliers get to talk to us and each other about what has been discussed during the day in an informal atmosphere. This helps back up the work of the day but is also a good relationship-building technique.

All in all the supplier days are good for us to help get the suppliers to understand our business and for them to be more focused in the areas that they can help us with. They are also good for the suppliers, in that it helps their business development to be more focused and can help them identify new opportunities with us.

Another technique we use is to include cooperation with other suppliers and innovation clauses in the contracts. These are difficult to enforce as legal clauses but their presence does give us some leverage if suppliers aren't playing nicely with each other.

One other technique is to not only maintain regular contact but to mix up the contacts. Rather than having operational–operational, commercial–commercial, CEO–CEO etc. contacts all the time, we get different people from ourselves and the supplier involved. As a general technique this raises the level of understanding of the wider issues for both us and the supplier, but it can also sometimes come up with unique solutions. A different perspective always helps.

o) If you are encouraging innovation from suppliers you have to be prepared to reward them for it. You want the supplier to innovate to help your organisation but there needs to be something in it for them. Keeping the client happy and helping to retain the business is certainly a benefit to the supplier but a more immediate reward is often warranted.

Some of the contracts we have with suppliers have a mechanism to share the benefit of improvements to the services. It is nearly always difficult to value improvements but if you have a good relationship between supplier and client you should be able to reach a mutually agreeable solution where the supplier receives an immediate financial benefit for the innovation they have brought to you but you also get some immediate benefit. Both of you gain.

p) Look for proactive remedies. These are now being pushed by the legal profession as a way of avoiding harsher contractual remedies (Fleetwood 2013). Rather than be faced with damages or termination there is the option of putting in place processes that identify risks and proactively manage them so that they do not reach the point of breach or damages. This proactive approach also reflects the reality that sometimes risks are out of the control of the parties to the contract.

Proactive remedies involve putting in place a process for assessing risk jointly and a process for agreeing an approach to that risk. It can't be too exact, as you don't know at the outset what the problems may be, but putting an agreed process in place is half the battle. As long as the rest of the agreement is working neither party wants to go to the termination stage so this is a mutually beneficial addition to the outsourcing arrangement.

q) Concentrate on the outputs from outsourcing contracts. Look more at the "what" than the "how". If you specify a service in too much detail in how it is done then you limit the supplier's ability to generate savings (savings which will benefit the client organisation) and you limit the supplier's ability to innovate.

Speaking from experience, suppliers prefer to be given outputs to meet and be left to their own devices on how those outputs are achieved. This allows them to use their experience and expertise to deliver a better service and to realise synergies and to innovate. If you are too proscriptive on how a service is run then you risk losing the advantages of outsourcing and end up with the in-house service being run by a third party and paying them a margin to do it.

This isn't to say that how the service will be delivered is of no interest to you. The client's experience of the service may show that the solution a supplier is suggesting won't work. Whilst suppliers can bring their own expertise the client needs to be sure their solution will deliver the outputs required.

It is also important for the client to understand how the service is being delivered. It shouldn't be a "black box" with the processes hidden from the client. At some point the client may need to step in to the contract and to do that it needs to know how the service is being run. However, knowing how the service is delivered is not the same as saying how it will be delivered.

Even taking into account the client's view of the how the service will be delivered, an output-based approach is essential for successful outsourcing and particularly multi-sourcing, where the larger number of supplier relationships means that an intrusive approach in how the service is provided may not even be possible.

As difficult as it may be the client does need to let go to a certain extent and let the supplier deliver the service in the way they think is best.

r)   Make sure you understand the objectives of the supplier. This is easily done during the tender process and I have found most suppliers to be very frank about their strategic and commercial objectives and their commercial restrictions.

If you understand their objectives you are in a much better position to judge whether they are aligned with yours. It is not absolutely essential that the objectives are aligned as, to a certain extent, you can manage differences and the level of alignment will very often depend on the service being outsourced. However if strategic objectives are aligned it makes life much easier.

s)   Don't get too hung up on service levels. Service levels usually only take effect after the problem has occurred and the penalties are usually capped. You are finding out about a problem after it has happened and your recourse is limited. Not an ideal situation for a dynamic service provision, and I am not the only one to think so (Martorelli 2011).

I am not saying you shouldn't have service levels. They help to define the service that you want. National Rail Enquiries will have them on systems for availability, response times, problem resolution etc. However they aren't that hung up on them and would prefer an engagement with their suppliers that gets issues raised and resolved before there is a breach of a service level.

t)   When you do have service levels, make sure that they are not only output-based but that the outputs fit with your targets. National Rail Enquiries have some service levels that are driven by external surveys on customer satisfaction and customer views.

These have to reflect what the supplier can control but if your aim is to keep your customers happy, it is not unreasonable to expect your suppliers to be measured on whether they are or not.

u)   Some clients are concerned about the outsourcer impressing with a lineup of experts in the tender process but taking these people away once the service has started. This isn't something I have ever been concerned about as my concern is generally what is delivered rather than who is doing it, but it can be frustrating when you have built a relationship with the outsourcer's staff throughout the tender process only to have then taken away when the service commences and having to start the relationship building all over again.

This isn't something you can contract against 100 per cent. It is not reasonable to expect the supplier to keep the same staff in place for the entire contract, as they need to give their staff career progression and can't keep people on the contract if those people don't want to stay there.

However you can offer some protection with a "key personnel" clause. This names people in the main roles and can mean that the client needs to be involved in the recruitment of replacements if needed.

It isn't a 100 per cent protection clause, but it does give some comfort that you will be involved in the selection of a replacement.

v)   Make sure you have a business case. Many of the failures in outsourcing come about through a poor or non-existent business case. Research by the Hackett Group (see SSON Editorial 2013) demonstrated IT implementations in the public sector were generally at the lower end of the equivalent private sector. They linked this with their finding that only 22 per cent of private sector technology initiatives were without a strong business case whilst the figure for the public sector was 70 per cent.

How can you expect to implement a successful outsourcing initiative if you don't have a clear idea of the expected outcomes and the benefits from those outcomes?

A clear idea of the business case, and a strong business case, will help a successful implementation.

w)   Align your outsourcing strategy with the business strategy. You can be successful in outsourcing but, if it isn't aligned to your business strategy, then you may fail overall.

This is not anything new. Strategic thinking is the key to a successful business and the various parts of the business should work towards that strategy. In this the parts of the business outsourced should be no different from the in-house parts.

x)   It is always a good idea to have "step in" rights in the contract. You may never want to have to exercise this right but you need to have the ability to step in and run the service yourself taking it away from the supplier, even if only for a short term, if the supplier really cannot deliver. Multi-sourcing helps your ability to exercise this right as in that model you are only taking over a small part of the service. However this right should be in all contracts. As a client you can't be in a situation where a supplier is not delivering a service and your only recourse is to sue for damages and retender. You need the ability to step in and take over the service.

Chapter 12
The Future?

Now I want to move into the possible future trends in outsourcing and here it does become opinion. Again I will use my recent experience at National Rail Enquiries, particularly in IT outsourcing but including other areas; however, it is all part of the build-up of information and experience over the years.

National Rail Enquiries is driven very much by the technology its users want to use. Twelve years ago it was all about person-to-person call centres, then it was the web, now it is moving to mobile channels. The National Rail Enquiries desktop website usage has been growing by 25–30 per cent for years, but in 2012–13 it grew by 2 per cent, and they expect 2013–14 to see a fall. Overall volumes are still rising sharply but they are more in the mobile internet and mobile app areas, where the number of contacts on mobile apps reached the same level as for the desktop site within 18 months of the apps first being released.

This change for them has two very different aspects from the move from call centre to desktop internet.

Firstly the mobile channel isn't homogenous. For a website you need to be compatible with different browsers and different operating systems but desktop internet is pretty standard. Mobile isn't like that – with different operating systems and devices, mobile internet, Apple iOS, Google Android, Blackberry, Windows, phone, smartphone, tablet, tablet mini etc., not only do you need a large number of versions to meet all the market, you also have old versions being dropped and new ones coming in with alarming rapidity.

The second difference revolves partly around the speed of change in systems but also in the increasing rise of customer expectations. With mobile, things are expected to be quick and your development cycle needs to reflect this.

So this means from the customer side you have a trend of a widening variety and an increasing speed of change.

Customer needs drive our business strategy and so our outsourcing strategy.

From the supplier side there is also an impact of technology. Yes there is a widening variety of platforms for user services but the systems are relatively well known and easy to work on. The Apple operating system iOS is used by many small developers, as is Android and the other smartphone operating systems. This means that the small app developers can now compete with the big multi-billion pound system integrators in delivering systems and software for relatively large clients.

Coupled with this is the increasing use of open-source software. The competitive edge that proprietary software gave to the big suppliers is being eroded.

In addition you have changes in hosting impacting on how you approach outsourcing. For example in order to build a website for a company that receives a large number of visits you used to have to go to a big supplier for hosting and software together. Now it is easier to split the services as it is simple to sign up with Amazon, Azure, Salesforce, etc. and get access to huge capacity and performance on a "pay as you go" basis. You can then go to a small boutique web designer to design your website but still get access to industrial-sized hosting capacity. Cloud is still relatively new and complex, but knowledge of it is increasing and there is support out there to help you make the transition.

In the past few years there has been a trend towards multi-sourcing, partly driven by the factors above. This is especially so in the public sector where there is a drive to introduce more work for SMEs and less for the oligopoly of large suppliers that currently exist. In an earlier chapter I covered the significant amount of public sector work run by the likes of Atos, Serco, G4S etc. I see the trend to multi-sourcing continuing and this presents challenges for suppliers and clients.

Suppliers will see average deal sizes fall. This isn't a bad thing overall as multi-sourcing does expand the supplier market. However they will have to adapt to be able to compete with smaller outsourcing suppliers in areas that have traditionally been the domain of the larger organisations. Larger suppliers will need to be able to provide the small, discrete services within their traditional organisation. We have already seen that with some of the suppliers at National Rail Enquiries. Multi-billion pound system integrators developing consumer apps alongside their traditional business of multi-million pound one-stop-shop systems delivery.

This trend also creates a challenge for the client as was discussed in Chapter 9 on multi-sourcing. Clients need to be geared up to govern these smaller contracts to get the full benefit. That involves rethinking your skillset and looking at what you need to do to manage the future.

I would like to illustrate this with an example, again, from National Rail Enquiries.

Whilst we have been multi-sourcing for quite a while we have generally left hosting with the application provider. The diagram below (Figure 12.1) could be the National Rail Enquiries website.

The first box could be the website user interface where the application supplier also hosts this part of the website. The second could be the journey planner where the hosting is in with the website user interface. The third could be the design company with the fourth being the static data (information on stations, train companies etc.) that is hosted by the application supplier. The fifth box could be the real-time predictions system where hosting is also with the application supplier, and so on. Some services, such as design, do not require separate hosting but if the service requires hosting it goes with the application contract.

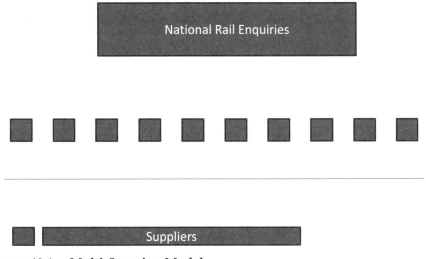

Figure 12.1   Multi-Sourcing Model

Planning Enquiries - Total

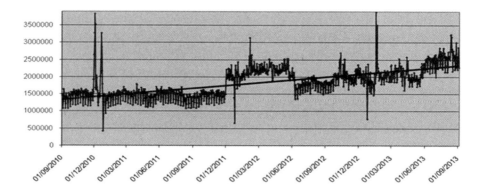

Figure 12.2   National Rail Enquiries Demand Issue

However the hosting being split across suppliers like this is not ideal.

The people running the applications are not necessarily experts in hosting and having several hosting operations is inherently inefficient with excess capacity in each area and not having the ability to gain volume synergies.

However for National Rail Enquiries we had a specific issue with demand that made this arrangement even more unsatisfactory.

Figure 12.2 shows journey plans each day for National Rail Enquiries over a three-year period. It is just journey plans so doesn't show the impact on the real-time and other systems. As you can see there is a general upwards trend with a daily volatility that gives a high and low with about 500,000 journey plans being the spread.

However you will also notice some major spikes both up and down. The downs are the Christmas period, where people tend to take leave – and also passenger trains do not run on Christmas day.

The spikes upwards are easily explainable but a little harder to predict. Take for example the spike up to 4 million from a run rate of just under 1.5 million in November 2010. This was caused by heavy snow, on a weekday, in the South East in England. Many people commute into London every day for work (around 750,000) and the train is the most common mode of transport.

When people wake up in the South East on a work day and see the world has turned white many of them will contact National Rail Enquiries. This may be by phone, web, mobile web, app, SMS, social media etc. but it all comes into the same systems. The same thing can happen with storms as was seen with the October 2013 storms in the south of the UK that severely disrupted rail travel. National Rail Enquiries had 3.5 million visits on 28 October 2013 (the day after the overnight storm brought a large number of trees down onto railway lines), 6.3 million journey plans (off the chart on the scale above) and 18 million requests for real-time information.

However it isn't just weather. The UK rail system is very safe but they do have accidents and they do have major delays, however rarely. These can occur at any time and have the same effect as snow but are even less predictable.

The National Rail Enquiries service can't be allowed to fall over so we set capacity at a very high level. Fine for the customer as the service is always there and hardly even slows down, but not so good for the service maintaining a high level of capacity all year round when it is hardly ever used.

What we needed was to combine the various hosting arrangements and have a service that flexed with our demand. I am of course talking about cloud hosting so when that service became popular we were very interested to move to it.

However, cloud hosting brings its own issues. The cloud suppliers are currently high in technology delivery and low in support. You need to be able to manage your services on their systems and do you own scaling of capacity. They will supply whatever you need but you need to tell them how much that is.

Because of the complexity of this we introduced a Service, Integration and Applications Management (SIAM) company into the mix. This is shown in the following diagram (Figure 12.3).

National Rail Enquiries holds all the contracts in this diagram but has the SIAM in place to triage problems and run the service desk side across hosting and applications. The SIAM also manages the migration of the applications to the cloud hosting and manages the capacity arrangements. With cloud there is considerable capacity available but you need to be able to scale up and down to make the best use of that capacity. That involves setting up auto-scaling and learning how to maximise the cost advantages of cloud hosting.

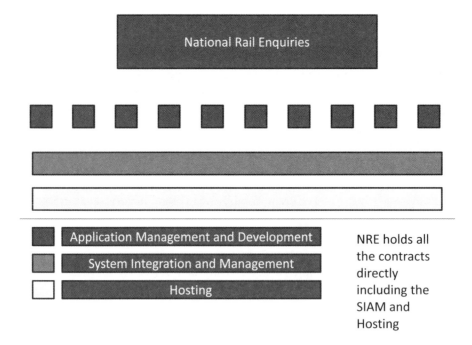

Figure 12.3   Multi-Sourcing with Cloud Hosting

That gives us the cost and flexibility benefits of cloud hosting with the service levels of a fully managed service.

This service integration model is one of the models Paul Corrall described (Corrall 2013) and is becoming more popular with a trend to more but smaller deals. It is also ideal for organisations moving to commodity-based hosting, such as cloud, where the service provided by the hosting provider is usually not that in-depth. Whilst the client still owns the service this is a highly technical and specialised area and some help in moving applications to the virtualised environment and managing the capacity and help desk issues can be helpful.

As well as things like cloud I see in the future a continued move to smaller deals and more multi-sourcing. As mentioned there is a big push for this in the public sector (they sometimes call it tower sourcing) to give more flexibility, help SMEs gain business and erode the oligopoly of the big suppliers. This will impact on the client side skill set as clients will need to develop the outsourcing skill set and move away from their traditional business skills. Governance will become more important and things such as the Life Cycle outsourcing framework will need to be incorporated into the client side thinking.

For clients this is going to be a paradigm shift, meaning a change in their way of thinking and operating. My experience is that there is a huge difference between single-sourcing and multi-sourcing. Not just in the technicalities but in the skill set required and the mindset of the client. The latter is one of the biggest shifts as you need to move from a relatively simplistic view of outsourcing to a holistic governance approach and with that comes the need for a different skill set.

This move will also involve changes for the suppliers. It will create a bigger market for the smaller players. The smaller deals will allow the small and medium enterprises to compete for work and use their flexibility and innovative skills to give them a competitive advantage. The UK Government have a target to have 25 per cent of its spend on goods and services going to Small and Medium Enterprises (SMEs) (Morse 2013b). This includes work done by SMEs through larger organisations but it does recognise the value these companies can bring.

At the other end of the scale, whilst there will still be the big contracts (it will take a while for the public sector to be in a position to fully embrace multi-sourcing), there will be a growing need for the big outsourcers to work on smaller discrete pieces of work as mentioned earlier. They will need to adapt to compete with the smaller companies that in a single-sourcing environment would have been subcontractors rather than competitors.

At both ends of the supplier scale there will be opportunities and threats. Suppliers need to recognise this and adapt.

This move to multi-sourcing may well see a rise in the systems integration and applications management organisations. Whilst it would not be single-sourcing, in some circumstances, such as National Rail Enquiries have found with cloud hosting, there may be a need to bring in a company to oversee a number of other suppliers to coordinate and optimise delivery of a service.

Summary

Through all these changes to the outsourcing landscape, be it cloud, SIAM, multi-sourcing etc., the underlying need for better governance of the outsourcing structure and suppliers is a common thread. This has been recognised in many industries, both in the public and private sector, and is slowly being actioned especially by initiatives from departments such as the Cabinet Office and Home Office. However the need is urgent as the governance needs to be designed as part of the outsourcing process rather than afterwards. As the framework in Chapter 10 shows, the governance develops through the outsourcing Life Cycle and touches each phase. That not only helps the phases but gets the governance process embedded in the minds and systems of the client and supplier. That is not so easy to do once the service is transitioned and then up and running.

Chapter 13
Conclusion

Nearly every company in the world outsources. From someone cleaning the windows in the office to an oil company getting a supplier to provide seismic surveys, provide the drilling equipment and test the well and reservoir, there is nearly always some degree of supplier reliance.

How you approach outsourcing and how far you take it depends very much on your business strategy. Outsourcing should be seen as part of that strategy rather than something you do to get rid of services that are problematic, or that you feel are not that relevant to your core business. You need to understand the advantages of outsourcing and what the downsides are. You need to have confidence that the advantages not only outweigh the disadvantages, but are advantages that help your overall business strategy. You need to approach an outsourcing strategy in a systematic way and to ensure that it is part of an overall strategy. You also need to ensure that your governance of your outsourcing is properly resourced and properly skilled up as well as following a plan. You can outsource some things like your cleaning without too much of a plan, but if you are embarking on a full-blown outsourcing strategy you need to make sure you approach it in the right way.

So a summary of my top 10 points would be:

1.   Make sure you understand the advantages and disadvantages of outsourcing before you do anything. As laid out in this book there are areas where outsourcing has advantages and disadvantages, which I have put into the categories of technical, human, strategic and financial. Look at these to see if they have a value to your business and take these into account, but look at the downsides as well as the upsides. It isn't all good news and you need to look at the advantages and disadvantages to see where it can help your business.

2.   Look at outsourcing in light of your overall business strategy. It isn't a separate business but a key part of your own, so if you are going down the outsourcing route in a serious way then you need to make sure that outsourcing, and the way you approach it, fits with your business strategy.

3.   Set an outsourcing model that suits your business. Single sourcing, multi sourcing, joint venture, offshoring etc. – whatever you choose, you should be comfortable that it is in line with your strategy and that you are prepared to put in the effort and the resources in order to make it work.

4.   Research the issue and don't be afraid to learn from others. It is more than likely that the path you choose will already have been trodden by others, so take the opportunity to learn from their experience. I have listed some techniques that I use and have seen used, and which may be of help, but there are a number of user forums and user organisations where you can learn from the experiences of others.

5.   Approach outsourcing with a framework in place such as the National Outsourcing Association Life Cycle. Your approach doesn't have to mirror the Life Cycle but it is advised to look at it as a basis for your approach.

6.   Resource up to manage outsourcing agreements. It is likely to require a different skill set from the one you already have, so don't assume that the manager of a department can still manage it effectively when the services it covers are being provided by an external supplier. You need the right skills and the right number of people. It is always tempting to try to cut back on the client side management overhead, to try to maximise the financial impact, but this is usually a short-term benefit. The cost of it going wrong is usually higher than the cost of managing it to go right.

7.   However, don't run the service for the supplier. The client side governance can be overdone, leading to a mirror organisation. You need to manage the supplier, not run its organisation.

8.   Having said that, you always need to be an active client. Don't expect it to just work. You have to put in the effort yourself to

make the service work and you can't just leave it all to the supplier. As I say repeatedly, it is still your service whether you deliver it yourself or whether you outsource it. You can't get away from that, so without running the service for the supplier, do try to manage the process and suppliers in an active and engaged way.

9.   Try to be output-based. Don't tell the supplier how to deliver the service. Tell them what you want the service to do and let them deliver it. If they are any good, they should only need outputs to aim for and, if given the freedom to decide on how to deliver the service, they may be able to realise synergies within the service and with other services they operate. It will also give them the freedom to innovate without a strict service description to hinder them.

10.   Finally, don't forget that it is still your business. This is easy to forget when you reach a stage where a supplier is providing a service to your end clients directly. However it must always be borne in mind that whilst the supplier is responsible to you for what they do, you are responsible to your clients and customers. Your clients probably won't care if a failure in your service to them came about because you were let down by a supplier. They will only care that there was a failure in the service.

Outsourcing gives you access to any number of competitive advantages in the areas of technology, speed of change, economies of scale, flexibility etc. – but you do have to approach it in the right frame of mind. There are enough examples of failures in outsourcing to make it pretty clear that if you don't think it through then it can really go wrong.

I hope this book helps in your approach to outsourcing and helps with the success of your business, whatever it may be.

Bibliography

Agar, E. (2003). Options for IT Outsourcing: Which One is Right for You? *Accounting Today*, 16 June 2003, 24–30.

Anand, N. (2013). To Outsource or Not to Outsource. *Outsource Magazine*, 33 (Autumn 2013), 62–6. Available at: http://europe.nxtbook.com/emp/outsource/Outsource_issue_33/, accessed 2 October 2013.

Barrett, D. (2013). G4S and Serco: Taxpayers Overcharged by Tens of Millions over Electronic Tagging. *The Telegraph*, 11 July 2013. Available at: http://www.telegraph.co.uk/news/uknews/crime/10173615/G4S-and-Serco-Taxpayers-overcharged-by-tens-of-millions-over-electronic-tagging.html, accessed 9 September 2013.

Bhattachaya, S., Behara, R. and Gundersen, D. (2003). Business Risk Perspectives on Information Systems Outsourcing. *International Journal of Accounting Information Systems*, 4(1), 75–93.

Birrell, I. (2013). Which Politician Will Dare Dismantle Crony Capitalism? *London Evening Standard*, 25 November 2013, 14.

Blatchford, K. and Gash, T. (2012). *Commissioning for Success: How to Avoid the Pitfalls of Open Public Services*. London: Institute for Government. Available at: http://www.instituteforgovernment.org.uk/sites/default/files/publications/Commissioning%20for%20success.pdf, accessed 2 October 2013.

Booty, L. (2013). The Problems with e-Health are Similar the World Over, Says Analyst. *Public Procurement Insider*, 18 October 2013. Available at: http://www.publicprocurementinsider.com/2013/10/18/the-problems-with-e-health-are-similar-the-world-over-says-analyst/, accessed 11 November 2013.

Buffo, E. (2004). *Reinventing Relationship Management*. Syosset, NY: The Outsourcing Institute.

Cameron, D. (2011). Speech on Open Public Services, 11 July 2011. Available at: https://www.gov.uk/government/speeches/speech-on-open-public-services, accessed 17 September 2013.

Claver, E., Gonzalez, R., Gasco, J. and Llopis, J. (2002). Information Systems Outsourcing: Reasons, Reservations and Success Factors. *Logistics Information Management*, 15(4), 294–308.

Clemons, E., Reddi, S. and Row, M. (1993). The Impact of Information Technology on the Organization of Economic Activity: The 'Move to the Middle' Hypothesis. *Journal of Management Information Systems*, 10(2), 9–36.

Community Justice Portal. (2007). A Guide to the Offender Management Act 2007 Regarding Probation Services. Available at: http://www.cjp.org.uk/publications/archive/a-guide-to-the-offender-management-act-2007-regarding-probation-services-27-09-2007/, accessed 9 September 2013.

Corrall, P. (2013). *Choosing the Right Sourcing Model*. National Outsourcing Association. Available at: http://www.noa.co.uk/files/304.pdf, accessed 23 September 2013.

Costa, C. (2001). Information Technology Outsourcing in Australia: A Literature Review. *Information Management & Computer Security*, 9(5), 213–24.

Currie, W. and Willcocks, J. (1998). *New Strategies In IT Outsourcing: Major Trends and Global Best Practices*. London: Business Intelligence.

Davidsen, D. (2013). Obama: 'Probably No Bigger Gap' between Private and Public Sector than Info Technology. *CNN*, 19 November 2013. Available at: http://politicalticker.blogs.cnn.com/2013/11/19/, accessed 4 December 2013.

Deloitte Consulting. (2005). Calling a Change in the Outsourcing Market: The Realities for the World's Largest Organizations. April 2005. Available at: http://www.deloitte.com/assets/Dcom-Luxembourg/Local%20Assets/Documents/Global_brochures/us_outsourcing_callingachange.pdf, accessed 16 June 2014.

Drtina, R. (1994). The Outsourcing Decision. *Management Accounting*, 75(9), 56–62.

Embleton, P. and Wright, P. (1998). A Practical Guide to Successful Outsourcing. *Empowerment in Organizations*, 6(3), 94–106.

Evans, P. and Wurster, T. (1997). Strategy and the New Economics of Information. *Harvard Business Review,* September–October 1997, 71–82.

Fill, C. and Visser, E. (2000). The Outsourcing Dilemma: A Composite Approach to the Make or Buy Decision. *Management Decision,* 38(1), 43–50.

Finlay, P.N. and King, R.M. (1999). IT Sourcing: A Research Framework. *International Journal of Technology Management,* 17(1/2), 109–28.

Fleetwood, B. (2013). Using Proactive Remedies to Solve Outsourcing Contract Problems. Available at: http://www.out-law.com/en/topics/tmt--sourcing/outsourcing/using-proactive-remedies-to-solve-outsourcing-contract-problems/, accessed 8 November 2013.

Flinders, K. (2013). IT Outsourcing has Changed, But Have You? Available at: http://www.computerweekly.com/feature/IT-Outsourcing-has-changed-but-have-you, accessed 12 November 2013.

Gantz, J. (1994). Outsourcing: The Scam May Be on You. *Computerworld,* 28(16), 41.

Gash, T. and Panchamia, N. (2013). *When to Contract: Which Service Features Affect the Ease of Government Contracting?* London: Institute for Government. Available at: http://www.instituteforgovernment.org.uk/sites/default/files/publications/When_to_contract.pdf, accessed 2 October 2013.

Gash, T. and Roos, T. (2012). *Choice and Competition in Public Services: Learning from History.* London: Institute for Government. Available at: http://www.instituteforgovernment.org.uk/sites/default/files/publications/Choice%20and%20competion%20in%20public%20services_0.pdf, accessed 2 October 2013.

Gash, T., Panchamia, N., Sims, S. and Hotson, L. (2013). *Making Public Service Markets Work: Professionalising Government's Approach to Commissioning and Market Stewardship.* London: Institute for Government. Available at: http://www.instituteforgovernment.org.uk/sites/default/files/publications/Making_public_service_markets_work_final_0.pdf, accessed 2 October 2013.

Goolsby, K. (2003). Impact of Best Practices in Outsourcing Arrangements. *Outsourcing Center.* Available at: http://www.egmanagedservices.com/wp-content/upload/2011/10/Impact_of_Best_Practices_in_Outsourcing_Arrangements.pdf, accessed 23 August 2013.

Halward, C. (2012). *Relationship Management – Art and Science?* National Outsourcing Association. Available at: http://www.noa.co.uk/files/300.pdf, accessed 12 November 2013.

Henry, D. (2002). Which Approach in IT Outsourcing? *American Banker*, 167 (9 August 2002), 9.

Heshmati, A. (2003). Productivity Growth, Efficiency and Outsourcing in Manufacturing and Service Industries. *Journal of Economic Surveys*, 17(1), 79–112.

Hickling, G. (2013). *The Ultimate Guv'nor*. National Outsourcing Association. Available at: http://www.noa.co.uk/files/303.pdf, accessed 7 October 2013.

Hill, S. (2000). Some Outsourcing Successes: The Pace of Technology Change is One Good Reason for Considering Applications Outsourcing for Your Next Implementation. *Manufacturing Systems*, 18(6), 34–42.

Hirschheim, R. and Lacity, M. (2000). The Myths and Realities of Information Technology Insourcing. *Communications of the ACM*, 43(2), 99–107.

Hodgson, R. (2013). *Public Sector Case Study: Department for Work and Pensions*. National Outsourcing Association. Available at: http://www.noa.co.uk/files/287.pdf, accessed 23 August 2013.

Hurley, M. (2001). IT Outsourcing: Managing the Key Asset. *Information Management and Computer Security*, 9(5), 243–9.

Hurley, M. and Costa, C. (2001). *The Blurring Boundary of the Organisation: Outsourcing Comes of Age*. Melbourne: KPMG Consulting.

Hurley, M. and Schaumann, F. (1997). KPMG Survey: The IT Outsourcing Decision. *Information Management and Computer Security*, 5(4), 126–32.

ICAEW. (2001). ASPs, Fad or Future. *Chartech Magazine*, 110 (February 2001).

Julius, D. (2008). *Public Services Industry Review – Understanding the Public Services Industry: How Big? How Good? Where Next?* London: Department for Business, Enterprise and Regulatory Reform.

Kakabadse, A. and Kakabadse, N. (2003). Outsourcing Best Practice: Transformational and Transactional Considerations. *Knowledge and Process Management*, 10(1), 60–71.

Kakabadse, N. and Kakabadse, A. (2000). Outsourcing: A Paradigm Shift. *Journal of Management Development*, 19(8), 670–728.

Kern, T. and Willcocks, L. (2002). Exploring Relationships in IT Outsourcing: The Interaction Approach. *European Journal of Information Systems*, 11(1), 3–19.

Lacity, M. and Hirschheim, R. (1993). The Information Systems Outsourcing Bandwagon. *MIT Sloan Management Review*, 35(1), 73–86.

Lacity, M., Willcocks, L. and Feeny, D. (1996). The Value of Selective IT Sourcing. *MIT Sloan Management Review*, 37(3), 13–25.

Langfield-Smith, K. and Smith, D. (2003). Management Control Systems and Trust in Outsourcing Relationships. *Management Accounting Research*, 14(3), 281–306.

Lankford, W.M. and Parsa, F. (1999). Outsourcing: A Primer. *Management Decision*, 37(4), 310–16.

Law, I. (1999). Harnessing Outsourcing for Business Advantage. *Financial Times Management Briefings*. London: FT Prentice Hall.

Lawrence, T. (2011). 10 Reasons Why Gainshare Fee Models Should be Avoided. *Proxima Blog*, 23 November 2011. Available at: http://info.proximagroup. com/buyingBlog/bid/71865/10-reasons-why-gain-share-fee-models-should-be-avoided, accessed 23 September 2013.

Lepeak, S., Beals, M., Campbell, L. and Moore, L. (2011). The Outsourcer's Guide to Success: Nine Factors for Successful Governance. *EquaTerra*. Available at: https://www.kpmg.com/DK/da/arrangementer/Documents/nine-factors-for-successful-governance-3008.pdf, accessed 10 November 2013.

Levins, J.W. (1996). IT Outsourcing: Heaven, Hell or Purgatory. *Journal of Bank Cost and Management Accounting*, 9(3), 27–47.

Loh, L. and Venkatramen, N. (1992). Diffusion of Information Technology Outsourcing: Influence Sources and the Kodak Effect. *Information Systems Research*, 3(4), 334–58.

Martin, S. (2012). IT Outsourcing Deals Gone Bad. *CIO Insight*, 31 July 2012. Available at: http://www.cioinsight.com/c/a/Outsourcing/IT-Outsourcing-Deals-Gone-Bad-851734/, accessed 23 August 2013.

Martorelli, B. (2011). Buyer's Guide: The Importance of Governance in Outsourcing IT Services. *Computer Weekly*, July 2011. Available at: http://www.computerweekly.com/feature/Forrester-Outsourcing-govenance, accessed 10 November 2013.

Mathe, H. and Perras, C. (1994). Successful Global Strategies for Service Companies. *Long Range Planning*, 27(1), 36–49.

McDougall, P. (2006). In Depth: When Outsourcing Goes Bad. *Information Week*, 16 June 2006. Available at: http://www.informationweek.com/in-depth-when-outsourcing-goes-bad/d/d-id/1044337, accessed 23 August 2013.

McFarlan, F.W. and Nolan, R.L. (1995). How to Manage an Outsourcing Alliance. *MIT Sloan Management Review*, 36(2), 9–23.

McIvor, R. (2000). A Practical Framework for Understanding the Outsourcing Process. *Supply Chain Management: An International Journal*, 5(1), 22–36.

Morse, A. (2013a). *Managing Government Suppliers*. Report by the Comptroller and Auditor General, National Audit Office, 12 November 2013. London: The Stationery Office. Available at: http://www.nao.org.uk/wp-content/uploads/2013/11/10298-001-Governments-managing-contractors-HC-811.pdf, accessed 25 November 2013.

Morse, A. (2013b). *The Role of Major Contractors in the Delivery of Public Services*. Report by the Comptroller and Auditor General, National Audit Office, 12 November 2013. London: The Stationery Office. Available at: http://www.nao.org.uk/wp-content/uploads/2013/11/10296-001-BOOK-ES.pdf, accessed 25 November 2013.

Moving On Up: Is the Recession Heralding a Return to Henry Ford's Model? (2009). *The Economist*, 27 March 2009. Available at: http://www.economist.com/node/13173671, accessed 2 October 2013.

National Outsourcing Association. (2012). *Lifecycle Model*. Available at: http://www.noa.co.uk/knowledge-centre/lifecycle-model/, accessed 23 August 2013.

National Outsourcing Association. (2013a). *Good Governance Best Practice Guide*. Available at: http://www.noa.co.uk/files/345.pdf, accessed 2 October 2013.

National Outsourcing Association. (2013b). Why Outsourcing Relationships Fail, and How to Make them Prosper. *Outsource Magazine*, 32 (Summer 2013), 60. Available at: http://europe.nxtbook.com/emp/outsource/Outsource_issue_32/, accessed 2 October 2013.

Overby, S. (2012). 4 New IT Outsourcing Pricing Models Gain Popularity. *CIO*, 13 April 2012. Available at: http://www.cio.com/article/704153/4_New_IT_Outsourcing_Pricing_Models_Gain_Popularity, accessed 23 September 2013.

PA Consulting. (2001). *Global IT Outsourcing, Strike the Balance of Global Leadership and Local Acceptance*.

PA Consulting. (2003a). *Outsourcing: Mindset Switch – Moving from Cost Control to Managing for Flexibility and Benefits Realization*. Results from the 2002 IT Outsourcing Survey. London: PA Consulting Group.

PA Consulting. (2003b). Managing the Outsource Relationship. Available at: http://www.outsourcingintelligencenetwork.com/oi_prod/images/oi_articles/Bestpractices/paconsultingmanagingtheoutsourcingrelationship.pdf.

Plavia, P. (1995). A Dialectic View of Information Systems Outsourcing: Pros and Cons. *Information and Management*, 29(5), 265–75.

Poppo, L. and Zenger, T. (2002). Do Formal Contracts and Relational Governance Function as Substitutes or Complements. *Strategic Management Journal*, 23(8), 707–25.

Quinn, J. and Hilmer, F. (1994). Strategic Outsourcing. *MIT Sloan Management Review*, 35(4), 43–56.

Raynor, M.E. and Littmann, D. (2003). Outsource IT, Not Value. *Optimize*, February 2003, 40–45.

Robotic Automation Software. (n.d.). *Wikipedia*. Available at: http://en.wikipedia. org/wiki/Robotic_automation, accessed 26 September 2013.

Saunders, C., Gebelt, M. and Hu, Q. (1997). Achieving Success in Information Systems Outsourcing. *California Management Review*, 39(2), 63–79.

Schwartz, E. (2008). Painful Lessons from IT Outsourcing Gone Bad. *InfoWorld*, 25 August 2008. Available at: http://www.infoworld.com/d/ adventures-in-it/painful-lessons-it-outsourcing-gone-bad-032, accessed 16 June 2014.

Skapinker, M. (2003). A Cost-Effective Way to Lose Control of Your Business. *Financial Times*, 15 October 2003, 8.

Social Impact Bond. (n.d.). *Wikipedia*. Available at: http://en.wikipedia.org/ wiki/Social_impact_bond, accessed 26 September 2013.

Sourcing Focus (2013). Serious Fraud Office to Investigate Serco and G4S. Available at: http://www.sourcingfocus.com/site/newsitem/serious_ fraud_office_to_investigate_serco_and_gfs/, accessed 8 November 2013.

SSON Editorial. (2013). What's the State of Technology in the Public Sector? Data from The Hackett Group, 2 December 2013. Available at: http://www. ssonetwork.com/technology-automation/articles/what-s-the-state-of-technology-in-the-public-secto/, accessed 4 December 2013.

Timmins, N. (2004). A Moving Story Minus the Tears and Trama. *Financial Times*, 5 August 2004.

Useem, M. and Harder, J. (2000). Leading Laterally in Company Outsourcing. *MIT Sloan Management Review*, 41(2), 25–36.

Vagadia, B. (2013). *Enterprise Governance: Driving Enterprise Performance Through Strategic Alignment*. Heidelberg: Springer Berlin.

Verizon. (2004). *Considerations in the Evaluation of IT as a Business Strategy: The IT Outsourcing Dilemma*. Verizon Information Technologies LLC.

Vitasek, K., Nyden, J. and Frydlinger, D. (2013). Vested Outsourcing. *Outsource Magazine*, 33 (Autumn 2013), 53–5. Available at: http://europe.nxtbook.com/ emp/outsource/Outsource_issue_33/, accessed 2 October 2013.

Whittington, R. (2001). *What is Strategy – And Does it Matter?* Andover: Cengage Learning EMEA.

Willcocks, L. (1994). *Collaborating to Compete: Towards Strategic Partnerships in IT Outsourcing?* Oxford: Oxford Institute of Information Management.

Willcocks, L., Fitzgerald, G. and Feeny, D. (1995). Outsourcing IT: The Strategic Implications. *Long Range Planning*, 28(5), 59–70.

Willcocks, L., Fitzgerald, G. and Lacity, M. (1996). To Outsource IT or Not? Recent Research on Economics and Evaluation Practice. *European Journal of Information Systems*, 5(3), 143–61.

Willcocks, L., Lacity, M. and Fitzgerald, G. (1995). Information Technology Outsourcing in Europe and the USA: Assessment Issues. *International Journal of Information Management*, 15(5), 333–51.

Zhu, Z., Hsu, K. and Lillie, J. (2001). Outsourcing – A Strategic Move: The Process and the Ingredients for Success. *Management Decision*, 39(5), 373–8.

Index

A Short Guide to Contract Risk
Helena Haapio and George J. Siedel
Paperback: 978-1-4094-4886-0
e-book PDF:978-1-4094-4887-7
e-book ePUB: 978-1-4094-7365-7

Partners for Good
Business, Government and the Third Sector
Tom Levitt
Hardback: 978-1-4094-3437-5
e-book PDF: 978-1-4094-3438-2
e-book ePUB: 978-1-4094-5942-2

Energy Management in Business
The Manager's Guide to Maximising and
Sustaining Energy Reduction
Kit Oung
Hardback: 978-1-4094-5245-4
e-book PDF: 978-1-4094-5246-1
e-book ePUB: 978-1-4724-0245-5

Finance for Purchasing Managers
Understanding the Financial Impact of Buying Decisions
Richard France
Hardback: 978-0-566-09171-1
e-book PDF: 978-1-4094-6419-8
e-book ePUB: 978-1-4094-6420-4

Visit **www.gowerpublishing.com** and

- search the entire catalogue of Gower books in print
- order titles online at 10% discount
- take advantage of special offers
- sign up for our monthly e-mail update service
- download free sample chapters from all recent titles
- download or order our catalogue